Bobby
Hemmt
The Gods Return

URBAN
VOODOO

URBAN VOODOO

A Beginner's Guide to Afro-Caribbean Magic

S. Jason Black &
Christopher S. Hyatt, Ph.D.

THE *Original* FALCON PRESS
TEMPE, ARIZONA, U.S.A.

International Standard Book Number: 978-1-935150-24-4
Library of Congress Catalog Card Number: 94-68556

First Edition 1995
Second printing 1998
Third printing 2000
Fourth printing 2010

Drawings and Cover Art by S. Jason Black
Edited by Steven Lang and Nancy Wasserman

The paper used in this publication meets the minimum requirements of the American National Standard for Permanence of Paper for Printed Library Materials Z39.48-1984

Address all inquiries to:
THE ORIGINAL FALCON PRESS
1753 East Broadway Road #101-277
Tempe, AZ 85282 U.S.A.

(or)
PO Box 3540
Silver Springs, NV 89429 U.S.A.

website: http://www.originalfalcon.com
email: info@originalfalcon.com

ACKNOWLEDGMENTS

A special thanks to Steven Lang and Nancy Wasserman for editing.

And to "Cici", a native Brazilian who, as a child was an initiate in *Macumba*. With her help, we were able to obtain information, both verbal and printed, not available in the United States or in English.

TABLE OF CONTENTS

PREFACE

THE PURPOSE OF THIS BOOK

In the past few years, the number of volumes on Afro-Caribbean magic has grown immensely. At one time the only books available either had been around for years (such as William Seabrook's *The Magic Island*, originally published in 1929 and Maya Deren's *Divine Horsemen* published in 1953), or were, published under the guise of ethnological studies (like *The Serpent and the Rainbow* by Wade Davis). An important exception was the excellent *Santeria* by Migene Gonzalez-Wippler. With the explosion of interest and practice, in Voodoo however, these books have proliferated. Many are, for the most part, repetitions of "scholarly studies," but with one important difference—on occasion some of the anthropologists and sociologists admit to having been raised in the tradition, and actively defend it rather than treat it simply as a "primitive" curio.

A number of small "spellbooks" have been published in English, but the bulk of this kind of material is available only in Spanish or Portuguese. *Urban Voodoo* is indeed about the practice of magic and spells, but more importantly it is written for the person born outside the Voodoo tradition—which is still often closed to outsiders—but interested in the practice. It is also focused on the frequently eerie experiences of the authors, who, like the reader, came in contact with Voodoo from outside.

While reference is made to history, this is emphatically not a history, but a handbook of practice and a record of personal experience. It is not the intention of the authors to "clean up" the practices to avoid offending the Judeo-Christian ethos—this book deals very frankly with psychic and psychological phenomena that some readers will find disturbing or simply will not believe. We assure you, however, that our experiences are not unique, and the history of both ethnology and psychic research is filled with similar accounts.

In the book we refer to the "Voodoo religions." We use this term to cover a variety of things that are inextricably intertwined: *Vaudun*, the Voodoo of Haiti; *Macumba*, one of the names for the Voodoo of Brazil; and *Santeria* or *Lucumi*, with its roots in Cuba. In theory these are all separate systems, but in reality this is simply not so. Some mention will also be made of *Palo Mayombe*, the black necromancy that has its roots in the Congo.

We would like to emphasize from the start that this material should in no way be considered simply "ethnic." It is an entirely New World form of magic originating in the Caribbean colonies. The emphasis of this book is on magic, and not religion or any system of social control or moralizing. While most white Americans think of Voodoo as black, in fact the vast majority of practitioners are Latin, or of mixed blood. There are an estimated five million practitioners in the United States, and at least a hundred million in the Western hemisphere. These are probably conservative guesses.

We decided to write this book for two reasons: first to describe the remarkable experiences and benefits we both gained from this most ancient and "pure" strain of magic, and also to encourage involvement by "outsiders" in what may prove to be the religion of the future.

S. Jason Black
Christopher S. Hyatt, Ph.D.

Note to the Reader: Shortly before this book went to press, a Santeria Church in Florida took their case to the Supreme Court of the United States and won the right to the undisturbed religious sacrifice of animals.

Be warned that police and Christian groups are expected to challenge this at every opportunity—legally or not.

INTRODUCTION

HOODOO WAR

S. Jason Black

About a year ago I was leaving the Grand Central Market in downtown Los Angeles. It was a rainy afternoon, and I was carrying about a zillion bags of groceries, so the moment I was outside I huddled against the wall away from the street as best I could. The Grand Central Market is an enormous enclosed space that covers a city block and is more or less the equivalent of a "farmers market." The fresh vegetables and baked goods are incredibly cheap so I made a habit of visiting it about once a month to stock up my freezer.

For the last twenty years or so, this particular section of downtown has become increasingly occupied by shops and markets owned by, or aimed at, the enormous Latin immigrant population of the area. These include not only Mexican residents, but an ever-increasing presence from Central and South America and from Cuba. If you hit the area on a Saturday or Sunday afternoon, you get the distinct feeling of being in some Brazilian marketplace.

At any rate, here am I, huddled against the wall by the corner, trying to stay dry. Having my hands full, and with nothing better to do, I turn and look at the display window of the drug store I was leaning against. My eyes stray across cold remedies, mouthwash, tampons, Voodoo dolls…

Voodoo dolls?

I haul myself and my zucchini into the store.

The place that I walked into is called the Million Dollar Pharmacy, and is on the corner of Broadway and Third. I suppose that it is indeed a pharmacy, and it is certainly a drugstore in the ordinary sense, but mostly it is something quite different.

Fully a third to a half of the store is taken up by what is politely referred to in the yellow pages as "religious goods." In other words, what was a pharmacy on the outside, was, on the inside, a Botanica—a supply shop for the practice of Voodoo and Brujeria.

There were racks of bagged dried herbs, candles in various recherché forms and tiny little talismans made from stamped metal, some of which I recognized, many of which I did not. There were floor washes and bath soaps to attract money or to destroy evil influence, good cigars for ritual use, racks of booklets in Spanish and Portuguese containing spells and incantations, and endearing little statues of Eleggua (more on him later) for home or office.

On the other side of the room were many seemingly orthodox items. There were crucifixes of various sizes in the baroque Catholic style, one or two rosaries and a glass case containing beautiful little statues of various saints. I already knew my subject, however, so I wasn't fooled by this show of Christian piety. The saints were all the "masks" of the various daemons of Afro-Caribbean magic, used as talismans and altarpieces by practitioners who don't want the local priest—or members of their family—to know what they are really into.

Below these were some striking items that I had never seen before. They were pyramid-shaped objects of cast Lucite containing carefully arranged cultic and talismanic objects that gave effect of sculptures suspended in colored air. These were obviously hand made and, upon study, I realized that they were talismans, each made for a specific purpose, such as money attraction. These seemed to be magical items, intended to be thought of as paperweights by the uninitiated. In much the same vein, there were Chinese Buddhas with similar magic symbols cast into them—another mask.

I walked out without buying anything—that time. While I was startled to have discovered that little wonderland in such an accidental way, especially after passing it a hundred times before, I wasn't all that surprised. Traveling between downtown and Hollywood—where I was living at the time—I could count around ten botanicas just on Sunset Boulevard as it led through the Boyle Heights district and Silverlake into Hollywood proper. In Los Angeles, as in cities like New York and Miami, businesses catering to *Santeria* and the various other Voodoo religions outnumber not only "occult" shops, but *Christian book stores* about five to one.

The weird thing about this is that, except for sociologists and "cult experts," almost no one outside the religions themselves *even know they exist.* This includes people who live cheek by jowl with these shops, and individuals, such as big city journalists, who should know better.

Example: A couple of years ago, I was watching the local evening news and the local anchorman appeared with a great big inverted pentagram bluescreened behind him. "Oh boy!" I thought, "Here comes some fun." There followed a report of what the newsman and the police both referred to as "Satanic rituals" being performed in the San Pedro area (a district near Los Angeles harbor with a large Hispanic population). The evidence for this included a rather sizable number of slaughtered chickens and maybe a goat or two in a dumpster. I was shocked. Not because of the alleged sacrifice of things people eat for lunch, but because they and the candles discovered along with them were obviously the remains of a *Santeria* celebration. Any magic that was involved was probably white as the driven snow. Yet, both our beloved Los Angeles Police Department and the professional journalists, both of whom should know better, never used any word but Satanism throughout the report. This in reference to a religion that I would guess conservatively to be half a million strong in Los Angeles county and with a much richer history.

My outrage at this demonstration of bigoted Christian ignorance was certainly in the minority, if not unique. Most of the W.A.S.P. population certainly didn't question the identification of this "outrage" (give me a break) as Satanism. In the Christian population, even in Los Angeles, the christening (sorry) of anything non-Christian as Satanism is a given. To a large extent this is also true among people with no particular religious affiliation or interest. Only a few people of European extraction are even aware of *Santeria* and its kin, much less sympathetic to it as I am.

Let me make myself clear. I have absolutely nothing against Satanism. I made it clear in a previous book (*Pacts with the Devil,* Falcon Press, Tempe, AZ: 1993 also co-authored with Dr. Hyatt) that it is a perfectly valid system of self-development and liberation along with the other forms of Goetic occultism handed down from our European ancestors. I *am* offended by the cowardly and emotionally crippling form of "Neo-Paganism" that today claims to be witchcraft.

What horrifies me is the use of the term as a weapon against a religious tradition who's roots were old when the myth of Moses was just being formulated.

There are comparatively few books in English on the Voodoo phenomenon from the point of view of the practitioner and most have been in print in one form or another for many years—the excellent and encyclopedic works of Migene Gonzalez-Wippler and Maya Deren, for example. Almost without exception, these books, including Ms. Wippler's, tend to whitewash certain aspects of the Voodoo magician's relationship to the world around him and attempt to make it palatable and acceptable to Christian society.

Dr. Hyatt and I have no such intention.

To begin with, we both know first-hand the futility of attempting to appease a fascist religious philosophy whose stated purpose for the last millennium has been the elimination of all other religions of the world. Over the course of time, this campaign of destruction has been expanded to include scholars, homosexuals, women, children, artists, and anyone displaying any talent in the area of human psychic functioning. This leaves a narrow spectrum of humanity—straight white males of no talent and small intelligence—who are acceptable in the eyes of "God."

If there is any question of what type I am referring to, just turn on the *700 Club* or one of its clones and there they are.

That vision of ultra-conservative loveliness, Pat Buchanan, has said that we are in the midst of a "cultural civil war." *We agree.*

Western culture in general, and the United States in particular, are in a situation that has struck Umberto Ecco as curiously similar to the Middle Ages. By this I mean that there are currently two or more distinct cultures, cultures with different goals, lifestyles, and religions that are *incapable of coexisting without violence.*

Please understand, I am not referring to some "racial problem." I am referring to the attack by what is known as the "Christian Right" on the civil rights—if not the very existence—of certain groups of people who will no longer submit to psychological disfigurement.

What has this to do with Voodoo? Simply this: of all the techniques of self-empowerment in history, there is practically only one that has survived the Inquisitorial onslaught and remained essentially intact and in harmony with its prehistoric roots: Voodoo.

Ripped by war and the slave trade from its ancient shores, it developed as a form of occult guerrilla warfare against a religio-military plague that spread across the planet. What we refer to as the "Voodoo religions"—Haitian Voodoo, *Santeria*, and *Macumba*—are now collectively one of the largest religions in the world.

And yet, in this country at least, almost no one has heard of it. In fact, on a recent episode of "The Mclaughlin Group" there was a commentary on the perennial troubles in Haiti. In a brief prologue they gave some statistics on the island nation. Among other things it was referred to as simply 80% Catholic.

This ridiculous lapse on a national news program (on which the lovely Pat Buchanan used to appear) was obviously due to Christian bigotry, pure and simple. Whoever had prepared the statistical segment couldn't bring themselves to call Voodoo a religion on television.

It is due both to this form of censorship and its own commitment to secrecy that Voodoo remains invisible to the population at large (in America at any rate).

We are talking about a secret society of sorcerers, with traditions old enough and numbers large enough to challenge the Judeo-Christian tyranny. This makes many of the segments of the "New Age" movement—whether we talk about followers of Crowley or so-called "Wiccans"—look irrelevant, something that the next several decades may ultimately prove them to be. They are, taken together, only a few thousands strong. Large enough to be noticed and persecuted, but not large enough to fight back. Nor, from my own extensive experience of these movements, are any of these people even remotely interested in the practice of magic, only in the practice of self-deception.

On the other hand, as I write this, an Afro-Caribbean religious group in Florida has brought their right to the religious sacrifice of animals before the Supreme Court of the United States—and won. It should be noted, as an aside, that at no time did the Jews have to appeal to the Supreme Court for permission to have a rabbi cut the throat of a chicken or cow and offer the blood to Jehovah. This, for those of you who don't know, is how kosher meats are made. So every time you bite into a Hebrew National hot-dog, you are partaking in part of a blood sacrifice. What an outrage! Call the police!

Since the Christian Right has declared war, this book is intended, in part at least, as a tool of guerrilla warfare.

Where the Judeo-Christian religions and most of the New Age movement tell you to repress your emotions and desires and to (pretend to) think "happy thoughts", we say, along with the ancient Voodoo gods, that desire is honorable, that anger may well be justified, that the will to power is nothing to be ashamed of.

This book partly tells the story of my involvement in the traditions of Voodoo and how it came about. There are stories to be told about "religious experiences" and "psychic phenomena", but each of these has, as its ultimate objective, "getting things done."

This book will not tell you that lust is "unspiritual" or that a money spell is "low magic." Nor will we tell you that curses are forbidden and will "rebound on the sender." All of this is rubbish promoted by failures who use the trappings of "spirituality" as a sop for their own inferiority; thus to them, lack of success, in a dizzying reversal, becomes proof of spiritual advancement.

The Voodoo gods are in the world, and to them the world is good, and so are the desires the world produces.

Many of the books I have read on Voodoo have, in a well-meaning, but pompous fashion, insisted that these practices should not be undertaken without initiation. We flatly deny this. This book is written from the point of view not of the *Houngan*—the community priest—but of the *Bocor*—the sorcerer. It is for the outsider raised in another tradition who may never see a *Santeria* priest in his life. It is for the lone practitioner, or the small group.

It is for guerrilla spiritual warfare against fascist religions that want you under their heels.

But especially, it's for getting things done.

We want to bring real magic, the genuine experience of the psychic and the supernatural, to the aspirant in the modern world. Here there is no need to dress in costumes from the covers of fantasy novels, or to try to "worship" deities fabricated by a potty old Englishman after World War II.

If you call, according to the formulae handed down from antiquity, I can assure you from my own experience when something answers you will not be able to write it off as "creative imagination" or "the experience of an archetype."

The magic works, and blends as nicely now, in the information age, as it did in the time of the schooner.

Maybe better.

CHAPTER ONE

INITIATION

S. Jason Black

I used to think that my "conversion" to the alien worldview of another time and culture was unique. I am, you see, of Scotch Irish ancestry and was raised in the Midwest. I was later to find that it was not unique at all, but almost stereotypical. It involved a series of weird experiences that bordered on (and sometimes leapt over the border of) the supernatural. After years of reading, I found that not only had a number of others of European extraction had very similar experiences, but the process was nearly traditional. Especially in Haiti and Brazil, people are often "selected" by the spirits rather than the other way around.

My "conversion" didn't come completely out of the blue. I had been involved in the serious practice of magic for a large portion of my life, the interest triggered by psychic experiences I had had since I was small. I emphasize *serious* practice. By this I mean things intended to produce tangible results or observable phenomena, such as the prediction of the future or the conjuration of spirits. These activities produced startling results with great regularity, or I would have given up the practice. By magic I definitely do *not* mean "Gnostic Masses" or "Drawing Down The Moon" or any other "religious" ritual that calls itself magic. These rituals may have some magical overtones but they are not the magic that we are speaking of.

First, a little prologue, to give some idea of the kinds of phenomena that I had experienced on a fairly routine basis:

About nine years ago I was residing in the city of Long Beach, a few miles south of Los Angeles. I was intensely bored with the place, and wanted to move north to the Hollywood area. To facilitate this I had taken a job in the Wilshire business district of Los Angeles, which meant an exhausting daily commute. Almost all I did was work and sleep, which kept me in a constant state of exhaustion. I tell you this to give some idea of my long-term physical and emotional state at the time—which has a great deal to do with the story.

I was working in a large office, dealing with crates of legal documents that had to be gone over and itemized for a corporate lawsuit, so as you can guess, the work was boring as well. Many of you have experienced the behavior that long-term boredom produces in an office. I am not referring to good-natured tomfoolery.

Among my co-workers there was a rather "Junoesque" (i.e., clinically obese) black woman who sat at the desk next to me. She put on a great show of being jovial and good-natured for the (absentee) supervisor, and then did whatever the hell she wanted to the rest of the time. The result of this tactic is that if a complaint is filed, the complainer is not believed, and further-more, labeled a troublemaker. I had already seen this, and so chose to remain silent when I became her target.

She was not my superior in the office hierarchy—it wasn't that kind of abusive behavior. It was the kind of thing that starts out as a few jokes at your expense and then escalates to open insults said deliberately within your hearing.

This woman's appetite for this kind of thing was greater than any I have since encountered. I had seen her do this to others, who, like myself, had hardly ever spoken to her, much less done anything to her.

This ordeal went on hour after hour, day after day, until, for one of the very few times in my life, I seriously considered physical violence. I was actually trying to calculate how much jail time I would get with no previous record if I disfigured her with a staple remover.

One day I nearly did it. I was so tired and her behavior was so vicious, that it literally took all my willpower not to attack her physically. For a few seconds my blood pressure was so high that, for the first time, I literally saw red.

During the long, slow ride home, part of my mind seemed to detach itself and go its own way without my volition. While still seeing what was around me, I was also watching a surreal little movie in my head, the images of which I quite literally had no control over.

In it, I saw a pair of hands (mine?) molding what appeared to be soft black wax into the lumpy form of what the woman at work would look like if I had the misfortune to see her naked. When this work was done, the hands took a box of pins and stuck them in the figure's stomach until it looked like a pincushion. Then I came back to myself. Except for some strange bodily sensations that accompanied this, and the bizarre sense that I was watching a movie that I could not control, I more or less dismissed the experience as idle imagination stimulated by anger and exhaustion.

I arrived home and, as usual, was in bed within an hour.

My eyes opened in the small hours of the morning. The luminous dial on my watch told me it was three a.m. I had awakened with the *sure knowledge* that something was going to happen to that woman during the next work day.

I had to get up at 5:30 a.m., so I returned to sleep as quickly as I could.

When the alarm went off before dawn, I could hardly move because of the interruption in my rest, but move I did. When I went out into the hall, I had a strange sense of foreboding. When I put my hand on the light switch to the living room, I froze. I stared into the living room darkness with the feeling that something was there, and that something was about to happen. I flipped the switch, and the bulb in the living room *exploded*. Not *popped*, like an ordinary bulb that burns out, but exploded into pieces. I could find nothing wrong with the lamp or the wiring. So, "big deal," you're thinking, right?

I dragged my hollow self to Los Angeles and then to work.

With bags under my eyes large enough for a winter wardrobe, I sit at my desk. SHE comes in and sits at the desk next to me. We work. Suddenly, I'm disturbed by a sharp cry of pain to my left. My evil genius has her chair pushed back, her eyes squeezed shut and her hands clutching her stomach.

Someone (not me) asks if she is OK. She complains of sharp pains in her stomach. They suggest she go lie down and she complies.

After half an hour, the pains have not subsided, and she goes home, not to return until the end of the following week. The story she told was this: the pains increased in intensity so she called her family doctor for an emergency appointment. His verdict was that he had no idea what was going on, and made arrangements for her to be checked into the hospital the same day. The hospital staff—according to her account—examined her, X-rayed her, and kept her under observation for three days until the pains passed, again, unable to find a cause.

Within two weeks of her return, she departed my office for a job at the post office.

Besides being an explanation of some of the problems of the U.S. Postal Service, this is one of the finest examples of "primitive" sympathetic magic that I have ever experienced. Except for the location in Los Angeles, and the fact that the doll was in my mind and not physical reality, this story could have come from one of those "Ju-Ju in my life" books British explorers used to write.

Two more first-hand accounts before the story of how I became involved in Afro-Caribbean magic, both classic: the love charm and the protective charm. Bear in mind that, as I tell these stories, I have deliberately chosen examples that had an *affect on the physical world*. I want to emphasize that I am not talking about "positive thinking" or "creative visualization," but something else that our culture does not accept. Bear in mind also, that whatever impression the following narration may give, I have not spent the last fifteen years of my life attempting to curse or bend people to my will. This, as I will make clear, is a great deal of work. But such stories make the best examples by their very nature. Tales of "spiritual advancement" often sound like, and often are, cases for the psych ward rather than theology.

Some years before I decided to move to Hollywoodland, I hung around with, and experimented magically with a young woman who was one of the best mediums I had ever encountered. She was a bass player/legal typist who could type 120 words per minute with no mistakes and was frequently wacky as a jay bird. She was also an aspiring poet with a sound knowledge of the Los Angeles underground scene. We had already done a lot of weird things together when she came to me with a kind of archetypal request, but one that I had never done on another person's behalf before. It turned out the side-effects were more interesting than the results.

She was one of those people who change boyfriends like some people change automobiles. And she was usually shopping for the next one while still attached to the first. So it was no great surprise when she told me she had just met someone that she already considered herself in love with. He was temperamentally rather conservative—hardly her usual type—so she couldn't just ask him for a vow of undying devotion, or make one herself, especially since she had only known him less than a week.

Since we had performed a few occult experiments that gave the appearance of producing results, she asked me if I would make a love talisman for her. I said that I would be glad to, but I had no way of obtaining a magical link with a man that I didn't know. That was no problem, she said, and produced from her purse a used condom that she waved blithely in front of my face.

After convincing her to please put the thing down, she also produced a carefully drawn love talisman from the *Key of Solomon*.

I laid out the necessary equipment (pentacles, incense etc.) and then we laid down a magic circle of protection.

For the most part the talismans described in the *Key of Solomon* are intended to attract a certain *class* of spirit rather than a specific angel or demon. Since this was the method she had chosen, I followed along in the correct manner according to the book and called on a venereal spirit in the name of several supposed higher intelligences. I instructed it to appear to the woman, and to compel her new paramour to commit himself to her in an unambiguous way. We spent some time in an auto-hypnotic state, willing the appropriate intelligence to hear the request and to manifest itself in the physical world.

Several days later, she phoned. She said that the object of her lust had intensified his attentions to her since the day after the conjuration and had asked her to move in with him. Apparently he had interspersed all of this with comments on his confusion at being so strongly attracted to someone normally not his type.

All of this can be dismissed, as with so many spells that "work," as something that was going to happen anyway, rather like the Egyptian priests commanding the Nile to rise in its season of flooding. I wasn't made aware of the really interesting part until she came by to visit the following weekend.

I asked her if there had been any "signs and wonders" of any sort following our ceremony, and, frowning, she said she thought there had been. She had had an intense hypnogogic experience while lying in bed that interesting state between sleeping and waking.

She had, she claimed, been visited by "monsters" that had tried to communicate with her, but had only been able to do so in a kind of pantomime. She described them as the sort of impossible mixture of species that one finds in ancient mythologies. At first I didn't see any connection between this experience and what we had done. Any old dream didn't become a psychic experience just because it followed on the heels of an act of ritual magic. However, something was nagging in the back of my mind when she described what seemed to be the principle beast that wanted to attract her attention. I asked her to draw a picture of it.

She made a quick sketch and a chill went down my spine. I went to my art portfolio, pulled something out, and showed it to her.

"Did it look like this?" I asked.

She got a shocked look on her face. "Yes!" she said, "That's it!"

What I had pulled out of storage was a painting I had done some years before, of a vision I had had during the evocation of a demon from the demonology called the "Goetia." The painting that I had done in no way matches the traditional description in the book itself and my friend had never, ever seen it. In point of fact, I hadn't even thought of it for quite some time, as the operation had had some rather frightening and unrequested results. We include both pictures here so that you may judge for yourself.

Here is the description of the demon and its offices from the *Goetia*:

> The thirteenth spirit is called Beleth. He is a terrible and mighty King. He rides upon a pale horse. Trumpets and other kinds of musical instruments play before him. He is very furious at his first appearance, that is, while the Exorcist lays his courage... This Great King Beleth causes all the love that may be, both of men and of women, until the Master exorcist has had his desire fulfilled. He is of the order of powers... etc., etc.

We took this little trick to be the communication of the spirit's presence that we had originally requested. It is not to be taken as proof that Beleth "really" exists—in the form of a King of Hell at any rate.

The argument over the existence or nonexistence of spirits will be taken up later in this book.

The "protection" story took place a few years earlier. I had not been long in Southern California from the Midwest, and was taking graduate courses at the local branch of the California University system. To support that activity I worked as a driver for a state-sponsored food program, similar to "meals on wheels." It operated out of the University food service so that I could work without destroying my school schedule.

The manager of the program was—to be polite—a highly strung woman that I almost never had to see. To make a long story short, I began to receive written "warnings" from her about work events that *never occurred*!

Or, when they had, they had happened to someone else. I quietly pointed this out to a supervisor beneath her in her office. The response I received (confidentially of course) was: "Oh, she's had a fight with her ex-husband. You'd better start sending out resumes." This did not seem responsive so I asked for an explanation.

I was told that she periodically had great rows with her ex-husband, who was one of my professors at the University. When this occurred, she routinely picked someone to fire in order to make herself feel better, and this time I was it.

I could not afford to accept this fate as it would essentially wreck my schedule of graduate work and, besides (goddammit!), it was completely unjustified. Of course, that was irrelevant.

At that time I was already heavily involved in experimentation with occult material supposedly given to the Elizabethan mathematician Dr. John Dee by "angels."

Of course, one must keep in mind that what a Renaissance religious theoretician means by angels is not what the average lay person means by the same word. During a successful conjuration—more of a seance really—I had had a clairvoyant vision which included a talisman to be made of raw clay, and instructions for its use (the details of this will be related later).

According to the instructions received, I fashioned the talisman from wet potter's clay and allowed it to dry. Then, early one morning before work, I placed it underneath the outdoor stairs leading to this woman's pre-fab office unit—the only way in or out. This—some of you will recognize—is typical of witchcraft techniques from every culture.

The result? After more than a decade at that job she quit, unexpectedly, and with only a week's notice. This occurred about three weeks after I planted the talisman, and only a few days before the first rain of the season dissolved it into nothing.

This story, I will be the first to admit, is far more circumstantial than the first two, and could easily be called "coincidence." However, there are two similar stories that I will relate later which are more striking.

All three of these events took place years before my experiences with "Voodoo" began, but they are excellent examples of the sort of phenomena that occur during the serious practice of magic. In fact, I would say that this sort of thing is "par for the course" if you take the trouble to do the work and follow the instructions—instructions which tend to be almost identical in magical texts and traditions from all parts of the world. The principle differences between Voodoo and the so-called "Western Tradition" is that, in spite of the travails of history, Afro-Caribbean magic has remained essentially intact in technique. The European material has been heavily censored and bowdlerized by its (principally Victorian) editors, with bogus notions of "karma" and other delusions about divine retribution culled principally from Theosophy and the Church. In no traditional magical system—oriental or occidental—does this nonsense exist in the original material. It is the self-defensive fantasy of a frightened middle-class mid-zonal mentality.

When I refer to "traditional" magical or esoteric systems I want the reader to understand that I am not referring to Wicca or the so-called Neo-Pagan movements, which tend to be largely based on bogus history or even (see Gerald Gardner) outright fraud.

CHAPTER TWO

WHITE ZOMBIE

My experiences with Voodoo began about 1983 or 1984. I had been involved with the "occult" for many years and had been in, or on the fringes of, a number of organized groups, particularly one based on the writings of Aleister Crowley. Out of frustration, I began to withdraw from these association. I had come to the growing, and disappointing, realization that while most so-called "magical orders" claimed to teach and practice magic, almost none of them did so. I must say, in justice, that for a period of more than two years, there was a core group who would drive long distances up to twice a week to spend hours in serious experiments. We worked with the "Enochian system" produced by Dr. John Dee in the sixteenth century. This work produced tangible results including "speaking in tongues," repeated poltergeist phenomena during some of the seances and the successful casting of "spells" using talismans clairvoyantly received.

Sadly, in time this practice stopped. What remained were the rote repetition of "classes" to new members, and the endless repetition of religious rituals, especially Crowley's "Gnostic Mass." With the death of the first organization's head in the U.S. the encouragement of many experimental practices decreased. Some members have declared the Gnostic Mass to be the "central ritual" of the order—whatever that means—and gradually some members came to believe that if you practiced the mass you were practicing magic. There are a few remarks by

29

Crowley used to justify this, but it is clear from his over-all writings that he never intended his occult training system to consist primarily of the Gnostic Mass.

All I can say is, that if *just* performing Crowley's mass makes you a magician, then every Episcopal or Presbyterian minister in the world is a magus.

And they ain't.

For those of you unfamiliar with it, the Gnostic Mass was written by Crowley as the communion ritual for his projected new religion of "Crowleyanity." It was based on the Episcopal high mass, with the Christian elements replaced with pagan ones and a tiny touch of the Black Mass thrown in for good measure. In places it is quite beautiful. In others it retains the tedium of the original.

The capper on my frustration came when, several years ago, I attended a performance of one of the "Rites of Eleusis" in the hills in California. These Rites are from Crowley's early attempts to recreate the ceremonies of classical paganism. When it was over I was sitting at a table with several people in casual conversation about the "Crowley's group" and other topics. I don't remember how it came up, but I recall expressing my disturbance at the apparent lack of experience by "initiates" of some years standing in occult practice of *any* kind, even in something as basic as yoga. I described some of my own experiences and I was told that no one had ever experienced anything like that. I then asked if anyone present had ever executed a ceremony of ritual magic. After a few moments of dead air, one man said that he had once done the Gnostic Mass. When I pointed out to him that that was more a *religious ritual*, he said "Oh. I was told it was magic."

That was pretty much the end—for a number of years—of my involvement with Crowley's group, although not with his writings and philosophy.

The point of all of this is simply that I had come to a personal dead end. As someone who had spent enormous time and energy exploring the processes of Western magic (by which I mean *practicing* it) this development filled me with disgust. It also pointed out to me a phenomenon I have seen repeatedly: the white European/Christian fear of the supernatural. The vast

majority of "occult orders" that I have come into contact ῾....
have found some way to avoid the very experiences for which
they are supposed to exist. In recent years I have come to call
these people "church ladies" since they pretend to be something
that they are not and create a fantasy world of identification and
comfort just like any of the Christian cults. (In contradistinction
to many Crowley and Golden Dawn groups, Chaos Magick
seems to hold hope for the serious student).

The result was that, probably like the majority of people
involved in esoteric disciplines, I began to practice alone or with
a very few selected partners.

I have had psychic experiences since I was quite small. In
fact, the inability of my Presbyterian minister or Sunday school
teachers to answer my questions about these (Presbyterianism is
radically non-mystical) was what started my interest in the
occult. During the intervening years I had become adept at tarot
card divination, astrology, pendulum dowsing, and trance work. I
spent a brief period as a professional psychic and a much longer
period giving readings for businesses (something I still do).

I mention this to make it clear to the reader that when the
events I am about to describe began, I was not in the least a
novice. I would also like to repeat that, at the time, I had no
interest in Voodoo whatsoever. What little I had read about it
rather turned me off.

I was sensing an impending change. I was working at a job in
the broadcasting industry for which I had had high hopes.
Unfortunately the business situation was going downhill, not just
for me, but for people all over the company. Promised promo-
tions did not take place, there was nasty in-fighting, the economy
sucked (it was the Reagan Prosperity Period) and one executive
who had just been moved from the east coast had resigned— "or
something." No one was sure, it was that kind of atmosphere.

One night in the midst of this, I performed a ritual to cleanse
the atmosphere, a basic pentagram ritual. (See *The Complete
Golden Dawn System of Magic*, Falcon Press, Phoenix, AZ:
1984) and performed an evocation of what I then considered to
be a "familiar spirit" called Orox.

I used a professionally made and balanced dowser's pendulum for basic communication during this exercise. The pendulum

gives positive/negative answers as well as measuring degrees of "intensity" regarding the subject inquired about.

I was informed that I had better be prepared for a move, since the situation I was in was unstable (big revelation—I already knew this). Furthermore, I was to get in touch with another energy—or order of beings, it was unclear—and what's more *they* were calling *me*. All of this was the result of an hour or more of probing with the pendulum, a process that was more than a little tedious.

For those of you who have no previous experience of this subject—either personally or through reading—this must already sound fishy. "Oh, right. They were *calling* him." For those of you with some knowledge of shamanic religious experience, this must sound familiar.

After the tedious process of getting this "revelation" I proceeded with the tedious process of finding out what the hell it meant. (People who pursue the occult for "the thrill" always tickle my funny bone.)

This was a simple process of elimination. Since I was dealing with a yes/no oracle, I needed a word or sentence to work from. I asked if a reference to what I was seeking existed in my personal library.

"Yes."

Was the reference in a fiction or non-fiction book?

"Non-fiction."

I then began, one by one, to name the reference books on my shelves until the pendulum indicated I had named the correct one. It was *Cults of The Shadow* by the British author Kenneth Grant.

I opened the table of contents and went through the same process until I was told what chapter to look in, and repeated it again with the page number and then with the paragraph.

Some of you may be thinking that the subject I was "directed to" should have been obvious to me once the book was selected. If so, you have not read the works of the fabulous Mr. Grant. Most of the later ones, including *Cults of The Shadow,* give the impression of being written in a state of frenzied delirium, with subjects that don't connect from paragraph to paragraph, and historical "facts" that he seems to fabricate on the spot. In many places it is such a word-salad that the oracle could have been directing me to almost any subject in the world.

As it was, it turned out to be something I would have to go out to research anyway.

The word—and the whole answer was reduced to something that small and specific—was *Ifa,* a *Yoruba* deity name that is mentioned only briefly in an early chapter of Grant's book. Mr. Grant claimed that this was the name of the "African Venus." What's more, I can say with absolute certainty that *Ifa* was mentioned in no other book I owned at the time.

"*Yorubas?*" I thought, "*Ifa?*" I thought, "For god's sake, *Venus?*" What has this to do with my problems?

I asked the pendulum if this was correct. It insisted, repeatedly, that it was. Having no reference that I could study, beyond Grant's few sentences that made no sense, I gave up on it for the night and went to bed.

The following evening after work I went to the Bodhi Tree bookstore in West Hollywood, one of the largest religious/occult bookstores in the country. I went there instead of the public library, having learned from repeated experience that if the library had ever had good references to a subject like Voodoo, they had already been stolen. Also I felt I might want to own my source of information.

Unfortunately, the selection of books on African religion or Voodoo were rather small that night, and what there was, was related to Haitian Voodoo, which is Dahomean not *Yoruban* (though there are many connections) with no references to poor old *Ifa,* whoever she was. I gave up in disgust and began browsing at random, putting the matter out of my mind. After a little while I picked up a (then) new book called *The Oracle of Geomancy* by Stephen Skinner.

For those of you not familiar with Geomancy, it is a rather complex form of divination which combines some of the symbols and forms of astrology with ancient "earth" magic. It was extensively used by Renaissance magi like Agrippa, and was part of the Golden Dawn curriculum. Dr. Hyatt has repeatedly informed me that Dr. Regardie used Geomantic Divination extensively.

While glancing at the introduction to the book, to my utter amazement I saw a complete description of the history of *Ifa*! *Ifa* was male, not female, and had nothing whatever to do with Venus. *Ifa* was a sort of "elder god" who had given both the gods and men the art of divination and then went about his business rather like the Greek Titans. He was also intimately involved with luck and with the performance of miracles. This was completely in line with my personal needs.

Except for the name, *everything in the Kenneth Grant book was totally incorrect.*

I emphasize this to point out the fact that not only had I no previous interest in this *Ifa*, but the only reference I had in my possession was utterly erroneous. This makes it less likely that my guidance to this subject "spouted from my unconscious."

A couple of evenings later, I performed a conjuration of "Ifa" using what little information I had. In European magic, as well as its Voodoo cousins, a "link" is usually formed with the spirit to be conjured using either a symbol or icon traditionally associated with it. (Full instructions will be given later in this book. Also see *Pacts with the Devil* (1993) and *Aleister Crowley's Illustrated Goetia* (1992) both from Falcon Press, Tempe, AZ). I had none of these traditional tools to work with, so I simply asked for some sort of "sign." I have done this before with some success, frequently receiving lucid dreams or weird synchronicities in response.

In this case, I began having dreams of floating figures that spoke to me, and exotic tropical landscapes I didn't recognize. Again, these were only dreams, and I don't present them as psychic phenomena, but they were noticeable as something unusual, and continued night after night for about a week.

I had purchased a book with some Voodoo material in it, but it referenced only Haitian Voodoo, and *Ifa* was not mentioned in that pantheon of spirits. This was another rather odd thing about the experience. What little I had ever read about Voodoo had been about Haiti. The tradition I was trying to find out about was, to my personal experience, utterly obscure. This further indicated that these "omens" were not cobbled together from my previous knowledge. It was soon to be driven home to me just how very little I knew about a world of magic that existed all around me.

I continued to perform my crude conjurations and tried to research my subject during the evening and while dealing with an increasingly chaotic office during the day. The only tangible results of my efforts seemed to be an increasing feeling of eeriness and tension, as though something were about to happen. Sometimes I had the feeling of being followed, which made me feel neither secure nor particularly sane.

The first certainty that I was having what the *hoi poloi* would call a "religious experience," and what I prefer to think of in paranormal terms, came on the third weekend after I began my magical experimentation. I was walking home alone quite late one night. I had just seen a movie at a local art house. For those who know Hollywood, I was on Franklin Avenue walking west from Vermont. This is an old residential area that was quite popular with movie people in the 1920s and still contains some impressive and well-maintained property. I wasn't nervous; I knew the area very well—I lived there—and there wasn't a potential mugger in sight. Just me and the skunks from Griffith Park. My mind was totally involved with the conjurations that I had been performing on almost a nightly basis, and I had decided that since—except for the dreams, which were not convincing enough—I had not received the requested "sign", I would drop the whole matter.

At the moment that I made that decision, I felt a crawling sensation along my skin, and the streetlights around me went out.

I stopped.

Telling myself to please not be a fool, I continued my walk, but the weird crawling sensation remained present. To calm myself down and also to test the situation, I said out loud, "If this is a spirit manifestation, then do it again." By this time I was two or three blocks away from the light failure and all the other streetlights were normal.

The moment I spoke those words, the lights on my block, and *only* on my block, went out.

This, to my mind, was starting to push coincidence, and my walk home became much speedier. By the time I reached the lobby of my apartment building I started to dismiss it again—

after all, streetlights went out in Los Angeles all the time. I stood waiting for the elevator to take me to my apartment and, when it appeared, since I still had the feeling of a "presence" I just said "OK, if you're there, do it again."

At that moment the elevator lights went out, and the elevator door began shuddering open and shut like a spastic colon.

I ran, did not walk, up the stairs to my home.

As an interesting aside nearly a year after the first draft of this book was written an article appeared in the Long Beach Press Telegram regarding a man who grew up in Beverly Hills and was told by several black musician friends that spirits were calling him. According to his story when he resisted this since it was alien to his background street lights would go out whenever he walked down the streets at night and this continued until he gave in and went to Africa to be initiated as a spirit medium. This man was also white.

CHAPTER THREE

THE GODS ARE ANGRY EFFENDI

By this time I became a little disturbed.

It wasn't that I hadn't experienced this sort of thing before—I had. If the practice of ceremonial magic hadn't produced this sort of result for me I would have lost interest years before (some of these events are related in an earlier book *Pacts with the Devil,* Falcon Press, Tempe, AZ: 1993). Nonetheless, interference with the city electrical system was new to me.

I continued to have frequent feelings of being followed or watched, as well as that odd crawling sensation on my skin. These feelings, incidentally, seem to be identical with the "vibrations" described by American and European mediums in the last century. I have felt them numerous times in relation to occult experiments. They have also been noted by the famous English writer on magic, Dion Fortune. They aren't really vibrations, of course, but that is certainly what they feel like.

While I had a sound knowledge of European esotericism, and had practiced yoga and other trance-inducing techniques, I felt increasingly that I didn't know what to expect from what I had "called up." Because of my years of study, I have rarely needed outside advice to deal with psychic or occult phenomena, but now I found myself casting around for some sort of knowledgeable human resource. I found it closer to home than I expected, in the form of an occult supply shop that was almost an institution in the area—the "House of Hermetic."

This was a nondescript (on the outside) but sizable store that catered to the occult and witchcraft community in the Hollywood area with books, candles fresh herbs and hand-blended incenses. I sought out one of the owners of the place and told him what had been happening to me. I didn't go into great detail, but I did mention that I had experienced what may have been "poltergeist phenomena." He had no problem with the story at all and implied that he had heard that sort of thing before. As well as Wicca and related practices, the store also catered to the local *Santeria* community, and he told me that he thought I might be having spontaneous contacts with the *Orishas*.

I think that I have made plain that at this point I didn't know what *Santeria* was, and for all I knew, an *Orisha* was a kind of fish.

He pointed out several books to me—especially the invaluable book *Santeria* by Migene Gonzalez-Wippler—made a few suggestions about how to behave toward the situation, and I left with my purchases.

After doing some reading, I constructed a crude altar—crude because I still hardly knew what colors or images to use—and began efforts to talk to "it."

I will refer to this phenomenon/concept/spirit simply as "it" both because of the ambiguities involved in any kind of spirit manifestation, and because I was still groping in the dark. And the only method of communication that "it" would respond to was the pendulum I had used originally.

Through the same sort of painstaking questioning described earlier, "it" communicated that it wanted a very specific altar arrangement and some tools that I did not possess. I was told that it required the figure of a head (see the section on Eleggua) and a set of divinatory tools called *obi* (instructions for this also later). The statue was not so problematical as the *obi,* since traditionally these were four lobes of cola nut. I don't know what *your* supermarket carries, but to this day I have been unable to find this item in Los Angeles. Sometimes four pieces of fresh coconut are used as a substitute, but keeping a divination tool in the refrigerator didn't appeal to me.

Not only did "it" tell me what to get, but where to get it. There were several large import stores in various parts of the area in which I lived, but to visit all of them would take all day, so I asked "it" in which specific place I could find what I needed. Not only was it correct, but on visiting the other stores over the course of the next week or so I saw that indeed the one I was directed to was the only one that carried what I needed. This sort of thing was to become commonplace.

I obtained a carved African head, with an extremely high forehead, rather like a UFOnaut from Kenya. Not only was this symbolically appropriate in my mind, but it was the only such bust that they had. I looked for shells as a substitute for the cola nut, since this is also a traditional divinatory tool, but found none. What I did find—and still use—were beads of flattened black glass of the sort put in aquariums or in arrangements of dried flowers.

In the seances with "it" that followed, I was instructed how to anoint the figure with perfumes (a practice I later discovered was common in Greek paganism) and how to use the *obi.* Two things are interesting here. The "spirit" flatly refused to communicate through tarot cards or the *I Ching,* both of which I had used for almost twenty years. I asked myself that if I was communicating with a part of my unconscious as some occultists theorize (or dogmatically state) why did "it" not use these? Why speak to me through an African system I had no knowledge of. "It" refused to have anything to do with this material for almost six months—as though it needed to *learn.* Secondly, I was to discover that the magicians of traditional peoples frequently walked off into the wilderness and returned with rituals, the power to heal, foretell the future, etc. with no access to books or teachers, but being instructed *directly by the spirits.*

Experiences like those described above, combined with recurring dreams, became so intense that I returned to the occult store to get a referral to a *Santeria* center where I could receive initiation. I felt so emotionally compelled by the experience that I was willing to present myself, your basic W.A.S.P., to a group of strangers in an alien ethnic subculture and ask to join the club, if—and I am not being facetious—we could even speak the same language. He told me that a *Santera* (*Santeria* priestess) was a regular customer and he would ask her advice. He was kind enough to follow through on his promise, and he took the trouble to call me at work with her response.

Her reply, roughly paraphrased, was: "Tell the white boy not to do it." I was rather surprised, not to say disappointed, but in years to come I was to find a few good reasons for her response. Despite the way it sounds these reasons were, for the most part, not based on race. She fully encouraged me to practice the magic on my own, but the *Santeria* community itself, even assuming I could have penetrated it at that state of my knowledge, was highly political and not altogether benign. They both felt I was too naive to get involved—and in time I came to agree.

In the meantime, in mundane life, I became part of a mass firing from an organization that, at the time, did not seem long for this world. I was far from happy, but not immediately worried because my savings, severance pay, and unemployment award were quite healthy. But not only were these the Reagan Prosperity years—when so many people fell out of the middle-class—but we were in the middle of the longest writer's guild strike in Hollywood history, so my other industry contacts were useless. They were laid off too!

CHAPTER FOUR

TELL MY HORSE—GO BACK TO MISSOURI

As you may remember from those wonderful years (around 1985), things got worse quickly. I must have interviewed at every talent agency still open (damn few) and several studios. The market, thanks to Reagan and the strike, was tighter than a new bride and my savings were slowly becoming cosmic ash. I continued my magical experiments, but I was "told" repeatedly that things were not getting better soon. In fact, I was warned of my firing through a dream the week it happened.

What happened was this: I had been assiduously avoiding making any "psychic predictions" regarding my personal situation. This was partly due to normal human cowardice, but mostly from a feeling of helplessness that, when the office situation deteriorated, there might not be any place to go. Readings that I had done for other people on similar topics had been depressingly accurate.

I went to bed one night after another dismal day watching the company hold on by its fingernails. I was presented with a dream in which I stood by a grave and watched a black coffin being lowered into the earth. When I woke up there was no question in my mind that this was my last week of work. I still hadn't been given any kind of notice, or even a hint, but then, neither had anybody else who had been axed. Sure enough, on Friday evening I was informed that that was it.

Months went by and I came to the genuinely horrifying conclusion that I was going to have to go home for a while until

41

the strike ended or something else happened to change things. I'm sure you know what I mean by "home"—that place we all leave in varying degrees of ecstatic relief. In my case, it meant a return to the Midwest after ten years in southern California.

In the middle of winter.

It was no consolation to me that a multitude of others were in the same boat. You may have seen some of the inhuman interest stories on *60 Minutes* and its sibling shows: grotesque interviews with mothers saying to the camera, "If he's living under my roof, he follows my rules. That means no girls in his room and no staying out after ten. I don't care if he *is* thirty-five." This usually with the humiliated son standing in the background.

As I was packing my possessions, I received a sort of benediction from the "spirit." It was only a few days from my departure. Most of my possessions had already been boxed for shipping and my airline reservations had been made. I still had my little "Voodoo altar" set up on a cloth on the floor printed with a Catholic religious scene. I was in the kitchen doing some final cleaning when I heard an impact and a light tinkling sound coming from the living room. I went to check on the noise, and saw a hole the size of a grade AAA grapefruit in one of the panels of my floor-to-ceiling windows. I thought that someone had thrown a rock and I turned to look for it.

Earlier I had done a tarot card reading for myself, in which, appropriately, the Devil and the Wheel of Fortune were prominent (those adept at tarot will find some little humor in this) and it was laid out in front of the African bust and other magical fetishes that I used. There was no rock, or baseball, or even a grapefruit.

What there was—its neck broken and its head laying square on the Devil trump—was a pure white dove. This is the part of the story some people simply don't believe—even people intimately familiar with "psychic phenomena." It sounds just a bit too much like a bad movie. Nevertheless, it is true. Those of you familiar with the traditions of both magic and paganism are aware of the significance of a white dove as a holy offering. Those of you familiar with urban areas know the odds against a white dove—as opposed to a pigeon—thinking my third story window was a piece of sky.

I tore its head off and drenched the bust and my instruments in its blood.

This is the place where people not raised in the tradition have problems: the blood offering. For now I will confine myself to the narrative, but since animal offerings are an integral part of Voodoo traditions, it will be discussed in greater detail later.

So home I went—luckily for a much shorter time than expected. About this four-month period there are two events related to our subject.

I have at times been asked, regarding the practice of any kind of magic, "what good does it do you really?" Hopefully this book will go a long way to answer that in concrete terms (as opposed to mystical nonsense). It has been my habit, for years before the "Voodoo" experiences began, to read the tarot cards every morning. I did this both for prognostication and as a mental exercise. As I said earlier, there was a six month period when "Ifa" would not respond through this system. This period had passed just before my move, and I was in the habit of speaking to the "spirit" through this technique as well as the pendulum.

The day before this occurrence I had made an appointment for a job interview. My plan was to stay in the Midwest just long enough to make some money, wait for the situation to change in California, and then return to civilization. In any case, I had this interview set up and went to bed early to make sure that I was fresh for it. I then had a rather intense nightmare in which I was in a serious automobile accident. This could have symbolized any number of things, so I wasn't alarmed.

After showering, I performed my usual morning ritual and asked (through the pendulum) if the spirit would predict the events of the day for me. It said that it would. I then asked if it would speak through the tarot. It refused. After questioning, the only oracle that it would speak through was the Chinese *I Ching,* an unusual choice, I thought, for an African spirit.

So I threw the *I Ching,* holding in my mind particularly the question of my afternoon interview. The answer I received was: hexagram twelve, "obstruction" changing to hexagram six, "contention." This did not bode well for the interview.

As you may have guessed, I had the traffic accident predicted in the dream and by the oracle. On top of that, my license was being renewed, so I spent several hours in jail while they tried to decide whether I was driving without a license or not (hence the hexagram "contention"). The irony in this, as in all such stories, is that if I had heeded the warning and stayed home that day, I would have had no proof that the prediction was genuine.

This disaster, too, passed, and I began to want out of the situation even more desperately than I thought I would. I began an operation to obtain a job that would allow me to make enough money to return to the coast. During these conjurations my distaste for the Midwest was uppermost in my mind.

The following week I received a letter from an agent I knew informing me of an opening at a management company in West Hollywood. I knew the man who owned the office, called, got the job, and was back in Los Angeles within three weeks.

CHAPTER FIVE

DEAD MEN WORK IN THE FIELDS OF HOLLYWOOD

I became established back in the Hollywood area and worked in an office in the fashionable Sunset Plaza district just outside of Beverly Hills. Once again I was able to spend my work time around actors and writers whose company I dearly loved. Unfortunately the man who owned the management company was a failed actor who turned his spectacularly mediocre talent to screaming at casting directors over the phone and finding scapegoats for the fact that he had no idea what he was doing. Don't get me wrong—he and I got along just fine. But having to breathe the effluvia of his daily rages was a little wearing. I will return to this point shortly.

Having settled, I resumed my magical experiments and the study of Afro-Caribbean magic. I had taken a bit of a break while I was away—try to find a well-stocked metaphysical bookstore in Kansas City.

I learned long ago that one of the most useful tools in any occult practice, whether dealing with "spirits" or direct work on the self, is the ability to go into trance. The simplest means of becoming adept at this is to learn the techniques of hypnosis. Surprisingly, only a few practitioners of my acquaintance have ever bothered with this, partly because they are unwilling to work to become adept at it—and it does require work—but also because of an almost Victorian superstitious fear.

45

The technique that I used, and still use, involves a lengthy trance induction—not using a tape by the way, the method is active not passive—followed by the attempt to communicate with the spirit or force I want. This has sometimes produced ecstatic psycho-physical states, spontaneous healings or "poltergeist" effects. Using this technique, at least four times a week, I attempted to improve communication with the spirit guide that I still vaguely thought of as "Ifa." Now *Ifa* is not, I discovered, considered to be one of the *Orishas*. That is, not normally a spirit that communicates with mankind directly (according to *Santeria* theology) and I had always thought that the identification of what I was talking to was a bit muddled. So my main goal was greater sensitivity as a medium, and cleaner, more direct communication.

One work day, after an evening spent in this kind of exercise, lunch hour came and I decided to spend part of it at one of the classier bookstores in town. I went in and began browsing. In the fiction section, I had the strange experience of becoming "stuck." I had idly picked up a copy of William Gibson's *Count Zero,* thumbed through it and put it back. I had never read any of Mr. Gibson's work—which I had associated with boring speculation about computers—and wasn't interested that day. I turned to leave the store, and couldn't. I literally couldn't bring myself to take that step out the door. I kept wandering around, watching my lunch hour trickle away. My back hurt, and I had to pee, but I still couldn't leave. Finally, with five minutes left in my lunch break, I went back, picked up *Count Zero,* bought it and left. I felt a physical pressure ease.

Later, when I began to read the book, I had one of those eerie sensations of being manipulated or tricked that are so common when dealing with spiritist phenomena. *Count Zero*—which takes place late in the next century—was indeed about computer technology, being one of the pioneer novels in the "cyberpunk" wave of science fiction. What I did not know when I bought the book, was that as part of the plot, the daemons of Haitian Voodoo manifested themselves in the worldwide computer net, called "cyberspace"—a technological equivalent of the astral plane of occult theory.

Early in the story there occurs a pun on my name in relationship to the Voodoo spirit *Legba*. It was so direct that if the author had been an acquaintance, I would have assumed it to have been a deliberate joke. I looked up Legba in my references and found that he was associated with exactly the sort of phenomena and talents that the spirit had manifested. During the next seance I asked if it was identifying itself as Legba. The answer was "yes." I asked for another "sign" to assure me my conclusions were correct. I had some errands to run, so I left home, and, while walking down the street, my eye was caught by something on the sidewalk. It was a dollar bill held down by a colorful bird feather and cowry shell that had been cut and filed to be part of a set of *caracoles*—the traditional divination system of *Santeria*. This was in an area swarming with street people, and yet it remained untouched until I picked it up. The shell, feather, and money together had the look of an *Ebbo*, an offering or spell to the spirits of Voodoo. I supposed I had my answer.

That was neither the first time nor the last that an important question was answered by strange synchronicities involving a book I had never read. Both Robert Anton Wilson and Colin Wilson have written about similar experiences in the course of their work.

Back at the office, my employer continued to scream into the telephone to camouflage his general lack of business acumen. Being around this eight hours a day was making me a nervous wreck. After a particularly bad day, I decided to see what could be done about it.

While he was out, I picked up one of his absent-mindedly scrawled notes and took it with me as a "magical link", that is, a personal object that theoretically maintains an Etheric link with the person who owned it.

At home I took the note to my altar and began the trance-induction and invocation ritual that had come to be my basic procedure. I placed the "link" underneath a drawing of the *veve* or graphic symbol of Legba and proceeded to make my request. I spoke out loud (and I think this is important) and explained the situation as though I were talking to another person in the room. In the tradition of Voodoo magic, especially the Haitian variety, there are techniques whereby another man's spirit can be "bound" with the help of familiar spirits, especially if he is considered to have behaved aggressively toward the magician. Basically, I requested that the man I worked for be constrained from making his crazy outbursts and behave like a civilized adult. I then placed the link underneath the talisman consecrated to Legba, and placed both in a small wooden box. I closed the ritual and went to sleep.

When he walked in the following morning, he had a glazed look in his eyes and he moved rather slowly, as though drugged. He complained of a lack of energy and fuzzy-headedness. He left early that day, thinking that he might be coming down with something.

He wasn't. From that day until I left for a better position three or four months later his behavior was completely changed. His outbursts almost completely disappeared. When I left I destroyed the magical link, and was later told that his old behavior patterns had returned.

Immediately after the successful manifestation of the spell, I began to feel rather tired myself. This was not a flu, but a general lowering of energy that I couldn't shake. It finally dawned on me that I had neglected to do what any *Santero* or Haitian *Bocor* would have done to start with: feed the spirit that was doing me the favor.

According to tradition, aside from the appropriate animal offerings that I did not have access to (it's hard to get a live chicken in the city) Legba was supposed to be appeased by the spine and tail bones of food animals. This was because, as lord of the roadways and information, the spinal cord which carries so many nerve impulses to and from the brain was within his natural province.

I went to a local market that catered to the Hispanic community, and which had a butcher who could provide out-of-the-ordinary cuts of meat. I bought a section of spinal cord which I placed on the altar. I asked if this was acceptable, and the answer was "yes." I asked (through the pendulum) how long it should remain. It said, "nine days." This did not thrill me, but I put the offering in a sealed container and followed instructions. The malaise from which I had suffered lifted instantly.

Psychosomatic? I can't argue the point. I know only that the phenomenon was not something I expected. The energy to cause the "magical" change I desired had to come from somewhere. Since I had not fed the spirit, he was obliged to take it from me.

All of this, I have to insist, was not coincidence, as it involved a personality change in my employer with no apparent cause and totally at variance with what had been for years his normal behavior. This followed, point for point, the requests I had made the evening before.

The more material I accumulated on the various Voodoo traditions—Haitian, *Santeria* and *Macumba*—the wider my experimentation went. I learned some of the traditional methods of Afro-Caribbean divination and tried to see if there was anything else floating around in the aether that would talk to me.

By this time I had departed to a large extent from the "psychological" view of spirit phenomena made popular in the last twenty years or so—the notion that it was all "the collective unconscious" or some such thing. I had come to the conclusion that the entire "Voodoo" experience began with me in the first place because—completely unbeknownst to me—I was living in an area where such things were practiced and those specific spirits—or things that answered to those names, were called up. In short, I lived in their neighborhood, and being an experienced medium, one of them came by to make my acquaintance. Maybe this sounds too literal to you. I will defend my position later.

I had identified what I considered a class or "family" of intelligences referred to in the Haitian tradition as Lords of the Crossroads—like Legba—and in *Macumba* as Eshus and in *Santeria* as Elegguas. All, it seemed to me, were different names for the same class of beings. I selected a spirit called Eshu Marabo, one that could perform healings, bring luck, defend the magician, and so forth. This was partly to further my career, but partly just to see what would happen. It became a rather cute, but frustrating, relationship with what religious historians refer to as "the trickster." The family of Eshus (sometimes spelled Exu) were generally considered devils, which made the whole thing even more attractive to me.

The *Orishas* of *Santeria* and *Macumba* are basically the same. They come from the *Yoruba* tradition while the Haitian spirits go by what are largely Dahomean names. From the Brazilian literature there is a whole constellation of graphic talismans and signs used in the magic. Most of this cannot be obtained in the U.S. and we will supply some of that obscure material in this book. One of the reasons I selected Eshu Marabo was that he was one of the few Eshus for whom I could find a magical signature.

I began with pendulum divination to decide what would be an appropriate way to propitiate the spirit. Somewhat to my horror, the oracle insisted on the heavy use of cigars rather than incense as a fumigant. As a lifelong non-smoker, I had visions of making myself sick at each conjuration, but this is what it said, so I went along.

None of the Voodoo traditions are purely African. The Carib Indians used tobacco in their rituals and this was picked up by the black slaves imported by the colonists. This, along with offerings of rum and perfume (which I was also instructed to use) have been an integral part of the magic ever since.

I performed the conjurations at least five times a week, requesting money, status, and a number of personal things. I must say that I was not impressed by the response to my specific requests, but there was enough genuine strangeness to make me believe that I had conjured something—Marabo or not.

I began seeing apparitions. These usually occurred at random times during the daylight hours. On one particular occasion, I was on my way to work, heading down the stairs of my apartment building, when, turning the corner at the stairway landing, I saw the figure of a man leaning over the railing above looking at me. I say the *figure* of a man, because that's all there was. He was transparent and a sort of tan or smoky color, like the hologram of a mannequin. I stopped, we "looked" at each other, and he faded away. The hallway was well lit with both light fixtures and the mid-morning summer light coming through a large nearby window. There were no shadows from people walking by—no one else was in the hallway. I looked at it for a long time—close to half a minute—before it disappeared. It was as if it wanted to be sure it had been seen.

While this was happening, a friend of mine, an experienced technician in the video industry, was being harassed by his employer. The strategy was apparently to force old personnel to resign so the company could avoid paying benefits. He was also involved with an occult group that I frequented and wanted to try an experiment to protect his situation. I told him to bring a "link" with the person or persons harassing him. I performed a ritual to ask what, exactly, to do for my friend. I was told that he should bring a potted plant as the focus for the "spell."

We met at the home of a mutual friend and performed a ritual of protection cobbled together from what I knew. He took the "link" and buried it in the potted earth. The spirit said that so long as he took care of the plant, his job would be intact and his persecutors would get retribution. According to his testimony, this worked.

I continued to make requests regarding my personal glorification and enrichment. These were answered in toweringly average terms. Strange things would happen but they seemed like efforts by an inferior spirit trying to appease me and look big—something of which many of the old magical texts warn.

For example, I requested money. As it happened, I also needed a new wallet. Walking in front of my office building I saw, laying on top of a newspaper vending machine, a brand new eelskin wallet, apparently never used. It was the same style and size of my old one, even to the color. Coincidence. Fine. But I had never seen a new wallet sitting in the open ignored by passersby as though it was invisible.

That same day, after work, I walked down the hill to the aforementioned Bodhi Tree bookstore. On the way, something caught my eye caught underneath the leg of a bus bench. I bent down to pick it up, and it was a ten dollar bill. I continued to the used book section of the Bodhi Tree and found a copy of a book that I had not seen in nearly twelve years, and never in that store. It was *Macumba, Teachings of Maria-Jose, Mother of the Gods,* by Serge Bramly. It cost ten dollars.

The frontispiece to chapter one was a graphic representation of one of the spirits. It was Eshu Marabo.

In addition to this, during one ritual, a stone weighing just under two pounds crawled slowly nearly a foot across a level altar table.

The final straw on all this utterly useless psychic silliness came when, frustrated at the lack of positive results, I asked what I could do to increase the spirit's power in the physical world. The response was that I should pile the altar with yams and smoke more cigars.

This was really too much. I dismissed the spirit and burned the related talismans, thanking it for the wallet and the book, and pointing out that it had done nothing that I requested.

It should be noted that yams are a traditional offering—along with animals—in both Afro-Caribbean magic, and in the original African religions. It should also be noted that during the period of this experiment—two months or more—I began to smoke more and more cigars during the ritual. I was and am not a smoker. I got the distinct feeling that the spirit—whatever it was—was using me to enjoy sensations that it couldn't, and tried to keep me satisfied with little tricks. This sort of thing is not unknown in either the occult literature or psychic research.

Do I think it was really "Eshu Marabo"? Probably not. People shouldn't put too much faith in conjurations or symbols on their own. I saw enough to think "something" was there. What it was I have no idea. Whatever it may have been, it was nothing I needed.

Eventually I went on to a "better position" than working in a personal management firm. I have to say that the improved position was due to an answered request from whatever it was that wanted to be called Legba. I performed the ritual as described and made a detailed request regarding money, location and atmosphere. I repeated this for several nights. Within the month I was informed by a director I knew of just the kind of opening I had requested. I interviewed after work and was immediately accepted for the job. The next day I was preparing to give notice, when the owner informed me that due to financial problems he was closing the office in a week.

I had been saved from trouble that I didn't even know was coming. This sense of "protection" or "good luck" has increased as time has gone by.

CHAPTER SIX

SPIRITS THAT FINDETH HIDDEN TREASURE

Up to now we have concentrated on "phenomena" and practical results rather than metaphysical theory. So few books on magic contain such accounts, because, I am afraid, many authors are non-practitioners. I know of several such—writing on anything from Crowley to the Golden Dawn to Wicca—who have never practiced magic in their lives. They usually justify this by confusing magic with religion, and by telling the reader that it's all a form of Jungian psychology, or quantum physics. This is called "psychologizing" or "scientizing" and are usually attempts by frightened people to make unfamiliar things familiar.

In my opinion this is fraudulent, although usually not consciously so. The truth is, the average Science of Mind practitioner practices more real magic than many self-proclaimed "initiates" or "adepts." This is not to say that there aren't individuals and groups that use these techniques to lead successful lives. There are; I have met them. But the cultural phenomenon of the "adept" who can't pay the rent and whose phone has been shut off for non-payment, is common enough that I had to point it out before proceeding. This book exists largely as an antidote to that attitude.

I had come to a time when I needed a sum of money rather badly. I had been laid off due to the slack season in the television industry and was living a bit tighter than I liked. Whatever my work options, I needed the money sooner rather than later. I did not need a tremendous sum: two thousand dollars would solve my problems nicely.

While I had manipulated job circumstances and created general runs of luck, I had never made a serious effort to produce raw cash—one of the prime subjects of the old Grimoires. Since I had a lot of time on my hands, I had nothing to lose in making this time-honored attempt.

I set up a more elaborate altar than usual (instructions for this later). While finding the appropriate candles I discovered that, due to the large Hispanic population, genuine *Santeria* candles could be found in the most surprising places—even supermarkets. Of course, most of the people who bought them thought that they were Catholic votive candles—although how they explained the one labeled "seven African powers" I have no idea.

After I had constructed the altar with what I considered to be the correct symbols and tools, I began each session with a full cleansing—or banishing ritual—based on the type described in the Golden Dawn, and censed the area of operation. I anointed the African head that was the "home" of the spirit with perfumed oil, and then induced an auto-hypnotic trance using a large piece of rock crystal as a visual focus.

Then I called up the spirit, and said exactly what I needed and why. Through the pendulum, the African *obi*, and the tarot, I would hold a "conversation" with the spirit. Answers to questions would pop into my head at unexpected moments.

I was "told" during a several day repetition of this lengthy exercise, that my layoff would continue for longer than expected (this turned out to be correct). Therefore, it said, I would have to make a direct appeal for the money as a gift. From whom, I would like to have known. Using the pendulum, I went through every option that I could think of. Finally, at a loss, the image of an aunt appeared in my mind. I asked if this was the person to approach. The response was "yes." I could hardly believe this because the woman was notoriously tight-fisted, and I would not have dreamed of requesting fifty dollars much less two thousand.

She, the oracle insisted, was the one.

In addition, the spirit insisted that the spell would not be successful unless a proper offering of "food" were made. It wanted the offering of a live animal, and would accept no other. After my experience with the cattle spine, I took this suggestion seriously. Since my options were rather limited, I obtained a "feeder rat" from a large pet supply store. These rodents are bred as food for large reptiles such as boas, and are available at low cost in many pet stores.

At this point, I am going to describe something that, at first, I had not intended to write about, but after some discussion with Dr. Hyatt, I decided that honesty was the most important thing, so here it is. In the tradition of Afro-Caribbean magic, especially of the darker variety, there are a number of spells involving the immolation of sacrificial animals in rather grisly ways. After many hours of seances with the pendulum and other devices, I was quite specifically told that the animal *must* be disposed of in a very specific way if the spell was to work. This required dropping the animal alive in a pot of boiling water. It sounds far worse than it was, and the animal died instantly, but I was in a sweat by the time it was over.

I cut its head off quickly with a very sharp knife, and spread the blood on the graphic image of Legba and the statue. Then I placed a tiny smear of blood on a postal envelope.

I carefully drafted a letter to my aunt. I consecrated the letter as a talisman by calling up Legba, asking his blessing, and, while holding the woman's image in my mind, telling him to travel with the letter to her home and touch her mind in my favor. I placed the letter in the blooded envelope, and mailed it.

The oracle continued to insist, in response to my repeated neurotic inquiry, that all would be well. As an additional test, I asked the pendulum when the money would arrive. It said exactly nine days. I noted the information and waited.

I received a phone call shortly thereafter from the aunt. To my complete shock, she had no objection to giving me the money. She was even willing to transfer it directly into my bank account. *And the money arrived in my hands in nine days—not just to the day, but literally to the hour—as predicted.*

On the grimmer side, the building I was living in had changed its "policy," which allowed a large number of people to become residents under what is known as "Section 8"—that is, on welfare. I have nothing but sympathy for people in this situation, but unfortunately, I was soon surrounded by violent types—the people who had moved next door were crack dealers.

I am libertarian enough not to object to such things on moral grounds. To do so would be complete hypocrisy considering my own experimentation with such things in the past. What I objected to was the violence. Every day I heard altercations, threats of murder, beatings, and the distinct sound of revolvers being loaded. I was once awakened out of a deep sleep by the sound of a person being violently knocked to the floor.

I spoke to the manager of the building, and she said she was in contact with the police. Nothing happened. I talked to the narcotics division of the police department. Nothing happened.

Then I had another of those warnings like the kind I received before the traffic accident.

One night I had a dream of a black woman crouching inside my open apartment door.

I woke up screaming.

Since I do not suffer from an inordinate fear of black women, it seemed to have been the open door that disturbed me. I got up, went to work (the layoff was over) and tried to forget about it.

I was proceeding with my magic and clairvoyant experiments, and the next time I performed my trance/ritual exercise, instead of the usual ecstatic feelings I had a feeling of foreboding. I asked the pendulum if I was being warned of something. "Yes," it said. I threw the *I Ching*.

Its response was: hexagram twenty-three, "splitting apart." Perhaps more significantly, in another translation it is called "stripping away." Those of you who have read Robert Anton Wilson's *Cosmic Trigger* or his *Illuminatus Trilogy* will be amused by this. As John Dillinger said, it was one of *those* coincidences.

The next day was a day off. I did my usual morning tarot reading and had the worst reading I have ever had, before or since. I have lost the note with the exact order of the cards, but I remember which cards came up.

Ten of Swords, Nine of Swords, Three of Swords, Five of Swords, Ten of Wands, The Tower, Five of Coins, Five of Cups, all rounded out with some court cards. Those of you familiar with tarot will realize that nearly the only negative cards left out of the reading were Death and the Devil and from my point of view these are not necessarily negative.

I had been warned four times in various ways that something bad was coming, supposedly on that very day. How did I deal with this? Of course! I talked myself out of it. This is our Judeo-Christian psychology at work. If you have clairvoyant talent, by the time you learn to use it, you've already been psychologically castrated. Anyone raised in a culture with psychic traditions intact would have known how to deal with the information. This, of course, is what European anthropologists and missionaries refer to as "superstition" and "magical thinking".

I had some shopping to do, and wanted to take in a movie. As I was preparing to leave, a man came to my door and informed me that he needed to do a little work on my ceiling. This seemed perfectly legitimate, as such work had been ongoing in the building for some time.

I left, telling him to lock the door when he left the apartment.

When I returned that evening, I found the knob—but not the deadbolt—locked. As I entered, I saw that I had been robbed.

Some electronics and some leather coats had been taken. Oddly, some art supplies were also stolen, but not the valuable stuff. What was enraging was the fact that the door had not been forced. After several days I concluded that the greasy little bastard that worked on my ceiling stayed until lunch hour, and not wanting to bother his supervisor, and not giving a damn, saved himself the trouble by leaving my door unlocked.

I also discovered—through the loose lips of the culprits—that it was the crack dealers next door who had done the job. They simply listened for the workman to leave for lunch, tested the door, went in and were out in five minutes. When questioned by the police, the workman's supervisor denied that any workman had even been on my floor that day.

I will save any comment about the incompetence of the Los Angeles Police Department (LAPD) for another place. Suffice it to say that reports were lost, and fingerprints were ignored.

So, while the police were busy gearing up for the Rodney King incident to come nearly a year later, I had to deal with the situation myself. I had, as I said, discovered who had done it. It didn't take Sherlock Holmes when all you had to do was listen to the ramblings of people fucked up on good crack and bad wine at 3 a.m., probably having been awake for four days straight.

I decided to try an old technique common to all forms of witchcraft. I went to the old Hollywood Memorial Park on Santa Monica Boulevard, and got a jar full of grave mold. As payment to the lords of the cemetery, I left a bottle of good rum high in the branches of a tree near the grave—it may be there still.

I took the material to my altar and prepared two talismans of a rather nasty nature. These were taken from *The Sacred Magic of Abramelin the Mage*, a Grimoire made popular by MacGregor Mathers and Aleister Crowley.

First I performed a ceremony to "charge" the material basis of the spell. Then I placed the two Abramelin talismans under the carpet in the hallway and, each day as I left for work, I scattered the grave mold before the doors of the people I wanted gone.

In addition I performed an evocation of one of the "lords of the cemetery," Baron Samedi or Baron Cimetere, or Baron LeCroix, whatever name you call him (or them, they may be brothers), registered my complaint with "him" and sent him into the next apartment to deal with the people who had wronged me.

Two weeks later, the man's wife left with their baby. This deprived him of his welfare benefits and thus, his rent. About two weeks later, my other target, the people across the hall who spent most of their time screaming, moved out. Not long after, the police finally decided to investigate the apartment next door—this was more that six months after the manager and I made our complaints—and all parties went to prison. Oddly, I was not involved in this in any way. I was not called to testify, nor did the authorities even speak to me. This was in spite of the fact that I made at least one written complaint to the police.

It was as if the reports to the police had disappeared. I was free of both the unpleasant company of my neighbors and the worry of gang retribution.

To avoid making this the autobiography of S. Jason Black, I will skip over some time and bring us to my connection with Falcon Press.

I had done some work for Falcon, was invited to work on a full-time basis, left Hollywood (with some relief) and moved south to the Long Beach area.

I began working with Dr. Hyatt on book production, the co-authorship of *Pacts with the Devil*, and several other projects. As the principal student of the late Dr. Israel Regardie, Dr. Hyatt had considerable experience in the practice of magic (as opposed to the pseudo-magic I mentioned earlier). Since we were living close together and had similar attitudes toward the subject, we began a series of experiments over an extended period.

These were primarily focused on the manifestation of money. Before you cringe at the pursuit of filthy lucre, let me explain the procedure we went through. Dr. Hyatt, as well as being a (retired) clinical psychologist is a licensed hypnotherapist. He is also the only person living who maintains the knowledge of Dr. Regardie's secret adaptation of Wilhelm Reich's orgone therapy techniques to in-depth magical practices.

Those familiar with methods of magic involving multiple practitioners are aware that usually one or more of the participants are designated as mediums. They either manifest the spirit to be called by full possession or through visions seen in a trance. Occasionally, the spirit will appear on its own, as an apparition, a ball of light or a poltergeist. I have seen this happen, as described earlier and in *Pacts with the Devil,* and have spoken to other people who have had similar experiences. As yet, I have no clue what conditions are necessary to cause this "classic" manifestation to occur.

I was to be the medium in this working. We began by using divination to decide what spirit or force to call up for our purposes. At the beginning of each ritual, Dr. Hyatt put me through Reichian manipulations for more than an hour. These are a series of breathing exercises (with no relation to Pranayama) and a kind of deep tissue massage. I do not mean to make this sound pleasant. It is not "massage" in the sense most people think of it—it hurt. But the method has the effect of loosening up and releasing psychological problems that have been locked up in the body. He followed this with an hour of Ericksonian hypnosis to increase my receptivity. Then we would proceed to the ceremony itself, beginning with a banishing ritual, and the casting of a circle.

All of this climaxed with the evocation of the spirit, a sacrificial offering in the Voodoo style, and the request to the spirit. The offering was usually either a dove purchased from a local bird farm, or a lobster that was killed on the altar and then cooked as a "communion meal."

I said "offering in the Voodoo style" but the truth is, this technique is common to all traditional magic. It is integral in such Grimoires as the *Constitution of Honorius* and the *Grand Grimoire* (both collected in *Pacts with the Devil*) and also in *The Greater Key of Solomon.* (The popular version of this book lacks this ritual because MacGregor Mathers decided to remove it, no doubt "for our own good." You can find the original material in both A.E. Waite and Idries Shah.)

We continued this operation once or twice a week—and it took a commitment of several hours each time—for about three months. After one early session Dr. Hyatt was awakened by voices and moving shadows in his apartment. He was so sure that his home had been invaded that he searched the apartment, gun in hand! He found nothing.

As a result of this work, money began coming in from completely unexpected sources. For example, a ranch that Dr. Hyatt owned was suddenly sold after lying dormant on the market for almost fifteen years. A Falcon Press book that had been repeatedly turned down by a Japanese company which had translated many Falcon titles was suddenly purchased. Along with the positive came what I call "trickster phenomena." We had a sense of an alien presence that, along with the help, took great joy in playing games. These games sometimes took the form of ghostly phenomena, but more frequently showed up as strange screw-ups in perfectly simple business processes.

For example, the international money order from the Japanese company was sent Priority Mail, and "lost" in the system for nearly two months. While we always got the money we asked for (except for Dr. Hyatt's request for twenty million dollars) we also got the sort of annoyance usually expected from dealing with a playful little child.

(Our definition of "magically" produced money was profit from sources so unlikely as to be bizarre, such as the sudden sale of the property which had been considered unsaleable for so many years. This, of course, was over and above usual business profits.)

Those who have read *Pacts with the Devil* are familiar with the ancient tradition of "making deals" with supernatural intelligences for protection and help. This was also part of the ritual process that we engaged in, and, even after the formal operations ceased, we both experienced windfalls just when we needed them. Dr. Hyatt experienced unusual "luck" on the precious metals market, and I received an unexpected inheritance that relieves me of monetary concerns for years to come.

For those who argue that this may all have been delusion and that magic had nothing to do with the events that followed, I can only say that I have given only the barest outline of the events. Further, Dr. Hyatt is a trained scientific observer and an expert statistician and his considered opinion was that the events following the ceremonies represented such a change in the current of events that it pushed well beyond "coincidence."

As a final addendum in this section of personal "wonder stories," I include one that, while not involving Voodoo per se, relates to one of the most important subjects in any tradition of magic: the existence or non-existence of spirits.

Around 1985, I was contacted by a friend of mine who had recently purchased a large Victorian gothic style house in Ontario, California. He had been a practitioner of Wicca for many years. He also belonged to the same Crowley group of which I was a member.

The house he purchased was built in 1889, and was one of the oldest in the Ontario community. It had a huge tree-lined circular drive, a beautiful view of the mountains—and a poltergeist.

His wife had been complaining of shadows on the wall— shadows with no people attached to them. Doors opened and closed by themselves, lights turned themselves on and off and something made at least one attempt to hang the cat. In addition to all of this, the animals (a basset hound, two cats and a cockatiel) would follow the movements of something invisible, all the while growling and hissing.

On coming home from work, he began to observe these things himself. He asked me to spend a weekend at the house to see if together we could at least talk to the thing, and perhaps, get rid of it. (There is a common theory that poltergeists are caused by disturbed adolescents but there were no children in the house.)

When I entered the house, my friend was still at work, and his wife showed me around. It was huge, with enormous ceilings. I immediately had a sense of being watched from a corner of the dining room ceiling, but, since I was being invited into a "haunted house" I dismissed this as suggestion.

My friend had told me that the center of activity was in the unfinished second story, so his wife took me up and unlocked the door. The windows had no curtains and the room was warm and brightly lit. I immediately felt that intense "buzzing" that I described earlier as "vibrations." I turned and said, "there's something in the far corner." At that moment a loud explosion sounded in the wall. This was one of those "rappings" that are famous in situations like this, and that, unfortunately, have also been a staple of fraudulent seance rooms. However, the genuine article has been recorded many times and examined in the laboratory. It does not have the same pattern as noise produced by striking one object with another, but the sound appears to be produced from within the solid itself, as though its very fabric were being manipulated. Thus the bizarre explosive or electronic quality to the "raps."

I thought this was just wonderful, so I said, "Please do that again."

It did. In the next moment I felt an impact by my right foot as though someone had slammed a blacksmith's mallet close to my toe. We returned quickly downstairs.

When my friend arrived a couple of hours later, I told him what I had seen and we both went upstairs to cast a traditional magic circle of protection. When all three of us were inside, the circle was sealed with prayers of protection and marked with a ritual sword in the medieval European fashion. By this time it was after dark, and there were two candles outside the circle as well as one inside to read by. We also had a tape recorder—in case of unusual sounds.

Soon after reading an invocation to command the spirit's presence, we all felt those "vibrations" and the flames of the two candles outside the circle began flaring up and then almost dying out. The windows had been nailed shut and no one felt a breeze.

Then we heard footsteps *stomping* up the front steps onto the wooden porch and kicking the front doors open. This was done with such force that it shook the house. The animals downstairs went wild.

I asked if they had locked the front doors, and they assured me they had. We sat in the circle, listening to the downstairs apparently being torn apart. We heard a sofa being thrown across the room, tables being overturned, and weirdest of all, a heavy door slamming just below us, shaking the floor. This in an archway where *there hadn't been a door for over twenty years.*

We repeated the magical invocation to control the spirit and demanded that it appear before us. It appeared above us instead. As the space we were in was only partly finished, there was no ceiling,—only the raw boards of the roof. Our attention was drawn upwards. From the roof over our heads came the sound of footsteps of a *very* large individual. As we watched and listened, we saw each individual board bend under the "footsteps."

When our companion decided that we had been duly impressed—and we had—the footsteps ceased. The attic area was still filled with a sense of presence. We quietly and politely asked that "it" cease annoying my friend's wife and attempting to hang the cat. We invited it to communicate with us if it had anything to say, retired downstairs and set up a Ouija board on the dining room table. It responded immediately and implied that it was a young daughter of the original builder of the house. Unfortunately my friend's wife began interfering in the process by creating a rather childish story of a woman who lost her baby and had been searching for it ever since. I asked her to stop feeding the spirit with her personal fantasies, but by this time, the ghost had found its patsy, and the operation was contaminated. In some annoyance, I ended the proceedings.

As a result of this, the phenomena almost completely ceased until about two weeks before my friend and his wife vacated the house. A search of the Ontario Hall of Records revealed that the builder of the house did indeed have a daughter and she had died in confinement in the house. She had developed severe *dementia praecox*—the old name for schizophrenia.

As a final note, when we returned downstairs to examine the damage, we found all the animals hiding in the darkest corners—but not a thing had been touched or moved.

CHAPTER SEVEN

VOODOO IN THE WAITING ROOM

Christopher S. Hyatt, Ph.D.

If all you want is peace and tranquillity, then die. Put an end to it now. Save yourself the torture of enchantment and disappointment. Save yourself the ecstasy and horror of meeting God in the flesh.   *The Curse of the Initiated*

W.B. Cannon's[1] article on Voodoo[2] death first attracted me to African religions.

I had read Cannon's article around 1963 or 1964 while I was an undergraduate student studying experimental psychology at California State University at Los Angeles.

Experimental psychology is sort of a mixture of psychology, physiology, inferential statistics and logical design problems. Although we did many experiments using human subjects, we also used animals. My experiments included social psychology, time perception, pain, sensory deprivation and brain implants. As you can see, the field is quite varied. It also offers a lot of latitude—if you can produce results.

Throughout my undergraduate and graduate career at Cal State, my professor gave me a lot of latitude. He was not the

---

[1]Voodoo Death, W.B. Cannon, *American Anthropologist*, 44: 169–81, 1942.

[2]For a detailed anthropological definition of Voodoo see: *The Serpent and the Rainbow*, Wade Davis, Simon & Schuster, New York: 1985.

usual specialist and had strong interests in magic as well as many other things. For my graduation he bought me a complete, uncut set of Frazer's *Golden Bough.* I got extra pleasure from reading this set since I had to cut every page by hand. Frazer's work intensified my interest in primitive religion but it was Cannon who I admired and respected the most.

Cannon's attempt to explain Voodoo death in terms of psychology and physiology fascinated me and led me to do further reading on the subject. Although I viewed Voodoo death (psychogenic death) from the point of view of a scientist, I was both horrified and fascinated by it. For years I had realized the power of suggestion. When I was fourteen I had attempted to use hypnosis[1] to entice a girl to have sex with me. Needless to say it didn't work. Although I failed, I never forgot the feeling of power it produced in me. To this day I remember it fondly. The horror of possession, whether real or imagined, has always fascinated me. Most people have a pull-push thing with being controlled. For some there is an erotic-sadomasochist quality. They fear it and are attracted to it. Voodoo is about possession and control and it appeared to be an *honest* religion since it was concerned with both practical results *and* spiritual development.

While it may sound naive, I thought that if religion[2] had any use, it was for man's betterment and joy, not for his enslavement. Voodoo seemed to fit that definition better than Christianity.

---

[1]Even today hypnosis is regarded as evil and dangerous. Although many respectable and qualified people practice hypnosis, it is still looked upon with suspicion. It wasn't until the 1990s that California repealed a law that prevented Marriage and Family Therapists from practicing hypnosis without special training. This law was intended to prevent Marriage and Family Counselors from using hypnosis to take advantage of their clients sexually. At least this is one claim. Another is that many of the people involved in creating the Marriage and Family Counselor licensing act were Christian Ministers at heart.

[2]The authors are aware that some experts do not regard Voodoo as a religion at all but rather as pure magic. It is our view that Voodoo is both religious and magical.

For an interesting and informative differentiation see Bronislaw Malinowski's *Magic, Science and Religion.* Both Malinowski and Frazer held that the move to spirits, demons and gods was a function

I never thought that one day I, a white man raised in the Christian-Judaic tradition, would participate in this ancient and forbidden religion. Later I was to find I was not alone.

THE INTRUSION OF VOODOO—A MIDDLE-CLASS NIGHTMARE

It was a cold and rainy Wednesday afternoon in Los Angeles. I was sitting in my consulting room[1] waiting for my next patient when the phone rang.

I hadn't heard from this fellow for a number of years and I wondered how he got my private phone number. We had gone to undergraduate school together and, while we both assumed we were friends, we were both very competitive especially over the affections of his flirtatious wife, Tara. You might say we were not friends at all, but two brothers competing for the affections of their childish mother.

After exchanging the usual formalities he got down to what he wanted. He was having difficulties with family. They had hired a women to help care for their child and do house work.

She was from the Caribbean and while a "devout" Catholic had "strange" and unusual customs. For example, she liked to buy live chickens and butcher them herself. This was no easy task in Los Angeles, even in the early 1970s. Even more strange, the woman would spend a lot of time in the kitchen stirring a pot that she would not allow anyone to touch. She would let people see it but not touch it. I asked my "friend" how old she was and he said, "About 23."

I asked, "Was she beautiful and would I like to date her." He laughed for a moment and said "yes" to the first part of the question and "no" to the second. The laughter seemed to break the ice a little. He said, "I want you to come over and see what

---

of man's realization that his own magical abilities did not work well enough. Thus, religion is born of impotency. Religion serves to provide hope and reduce fear. Many anthropologists believe that the differences between magic and religion are, at best, fuzzy.

[1] I had given up my academic interest in experimental psychology. There was no money in it and I didn't like the politics in the academic world. I was later to find out that the politics in the clinical arena was much worse.

she is about to do. You won't be disappointed. And by the way you will get to see Tara. She has changed a lot."

I told him that I was expecting a patient who was somewhat unreliable and if he didn't show up in half an hour I would be over. When he gave me the address I realized that he lived in a dangerous area, complete with gangs, prostitutes and drug dealers. I felt anxious about going.

The half-hour went by and, despite what I had promised my "friend", I decided to wait another ten minutes. I gave myself the excuse that maybe the weather had delayed my patient, but I was all too aware that my fear was the real issue.

Although I was brought up in a fairly violent neighborhood and had lived "in the streets" with all types of people, my years in University and my recently acquired middle-class values had turned me into a "chicken." I slowly gathered myself together and headed toward my car. All the time I was thinking about how I would stand out in this neighborhood. I worried about my car as well as my person.

As I headed to the ghetto my mind went to other things. I thought of my wife waiting for me at home with dinner. I had called and told her that I was hung up at the office. What would she think if she knew the truth? She knew how I felt about Tara and rightfully felt threatened.

My car pulled up to a set of large buildings. They looked like a barracks or a prison compound. There were probably twenty different buildings. They all looked drab and ugly.

I saw a beautiful woman walking by one of the buildings. She was dressed like a prostitute and had a man pinned to her side. Young men were quickly hustling up and down the street, stopping, exchanging packages and money.

Cars were moving all around me. The police had a strong presence which first reassured me. Then the thought ran through my mind that the police could just as well hassle or arrest me. As I wandered through the maze of buildings slowly repeating the building and apartment number to myself like a mantra, I looked up and found myself staring in the eyes of my "friend" who was anxiously waiting for me at the door step.

We shook hands and smiled at each other for a second or two. Our eyes darted away from our awkward glance and we moved quickly into a dark living room with the most awful smell. There were a lot of people milling around. I made out the image of his wife huddled in a corner. I approached her slowly. Her eyes were glazed over. She looked really stoned. She acknowledged me, mumbled a few words, giggled and went back to her staring and rocking. I felt frightened by how she looked.

He took me into the kitchen and introduced me to the girl. She was in fact beautiful and I was attracted to her. However, I can't say the feeling was mutual. She sort of growled at me and nudged me back a foot or so.

I left the kitchen. My friend told me that she was preparing "something" to get even with her lover. He had left her for another woman and took some of her money. She was fuming mad. I tried to ask a question but was quickly silenced by the stare of a big black man.

Strange sounds were coming from the kitchen, like the sound of flapping wings. In the dim candle light I could barely make out what she was doing. If my eyes didn't deceive me she was cutting off the head of a chicken while she chanted over a pot. She appeared to squirt the blood into the pot.

The pot was no bigger than one used to make soup. Maybe it held three or four quarts of water. This is just a guess. With the smell of grass, the beat of jungle drums, the candles flickering, the women gyrating, the big black man staring and the jumping chicken I was not a reliable witness. I was tense but still not anxious enough to ask for a drink. I asked my friend how he could let himself get into a situation like this. He simply smiled as he took another hit on his joint. He passed it to me but I refused. My middle-class imagination already had me losing my license and being publicly disgraced. Boy, had I become a chicken. At one time this would have been fun.

For a moment or two everything seemed to stop. The candles blinked, the music stopped and the "witch" seemed to disappear. I looked around and couldn't find her. I looked back into the kitchen and she was standing right where she had always been.

She seemed more relaxed. No, less tense. She motioned for my friend to come into the kitchen and see what she had made. He moved forward, grabbing my elbow and dragging me along. He looked into the pot and smiled. He motioned for me to come closer. I hesitated for a moment but noticed the big black man behind me—I quickly moved forward.

I stared into the pot[1] and was amazed and horrified. I saw the indented shape of a human form with a small needle in its heart and a drop of blood. My mind quickly raced around trying to find an explanation. I stopped thinking quickly enough, as I brushed a feather off my nose, and observed that the figure was not a positive image but a negative one. That is, it was imbedded into a burnt, dark, silvery dust-like material. The material was like coal with the texture of crumpled up aluminum foil. I asked permission to touch it and was refused. The negative human form had a protruding penis. There was a drop of blood on it.

Everyone, including the young woman, left the kitchen and returned to whatever they were doing. It crossed my mind to strike up a conversation with this women but I thought better of it. She seemed to read my mind and said, "You, white man, call it Voodoo," and she laughed.

I talked to my friend a day or two later and asked him how he got himself into such a strange situation and no wonder he was having trouble with his family. He said, "Don't jump to too many conclusions. I just thought you would be interested. Remember how fascinated you were with Voodoo and Voodoo death in college?"

I replied, "Yes, but living with this sort of stuff is another thing. It's not your way. You used to have so much class. And your wife was a joy. Now she looks like a zombie." There was silence on the phone. He said, "I thought I was doing you a favor, oh well." He hung up.

I laughed at myself for using the word "zombie." I thought she was just a drugged-out hippie. It always struck me how zombie-like certain drug users look. I hadn't yet heard of Wade Davis or zombie powder. After all, he didn't finish his Ph.D.

---

[1]The pot was not the infamous Nganga pot referred to in, for example, *Buried Secrets*, Edward Humes, Signet, New York: 1992.

dissertation until 1986[1] and I hadn't heard of *The S
The Rainbow.*[2]

I couldn't get "the witch" out of my mind. I had some ~~obses~~
sive attraction to her. I finished my day of patients, went home
and slept fitfully.

The next morning I had some difficulty trying to recall my
dreams. Instead of dream material, a number of memories of my
childhood appeared. I recalled how I used to stick pins into bugs
and imagine the bugs were my enemies or my parents. I remembered torturing a cat and calling it by someone else's name.

During the day other thoughts intruded. Like how I used to
pray to God to kill my enemies.[3] No one had taught me these
things. I made them up myself.

I thought, "How was what I was doing different from what the
crazy witch in the kitchen was doing?" Maybe the difference was
that her magic worked and my childish attempts to be potent
with my enemies were failures. "Yes," I thought, "all of this
behavior, hers as well as mine, was an attempt to be potent—to
cause effects when no other way appeared possible or desirable."
In my childish way I was practicing an organic, primitive
religion.[4] I thought, "Maybe Voodoo was the first primal
religion. I, however, didn't succeed, while she might. As a white
man, I felt guilty over my death chants even twenty years later
while she didn't.

My next run in with Voodoo came a year or so later when I
interviewed a mulatto women who was suffering from anxiety
and depression. She was from Haiti I believe and worked as a

---

[1] *The Ethnobiology of the Haitian Zombie (Ethnobotany, Voudoun, and
Tetrodotoxin),* Wade E. Davis, Harvard University: 1986.

[2] *The Serpent and The Rainbow*, Wade Davis, Simon & Schuster, New
York: 1985.

[3] According to Freudian theory death wishes are common among
children. During twelve years of practice I found that at least one-third
of my patients had difficulty admitting them. I believe that the death
wish is common to adults as well, but is well repressed.

[4] The use of the word "primitive" is not intended to imply that modern
religions are an advancement over what preceded them. To the
contrary, I believe they are not.

prostitute. She was a Catholic and very attractive. She, too, had been jilted by a lover. Her girlfriend, who was also a prostitute, told her to see me. I had a reputation for dealing with weird people and things. I also had a very middle-class practice and it was sometimes difficult keeping the real weird ones away from the normal crazy ones. Often I had to stay late in the office or arrive very early in the morning to perform this juggling act.

One evening around ten she showed up for her appointment. She held a large bag close to her chest. She was also smiling. "I might not have to see you for much longer," she said. "I think I found my way." She dipped into the bag and pulled out a doll. The hand-made primitive doll had blond hair and blue eyes and had pins stuck into its heart and its genitals. I knew what it was right away. When she saw my horror she laughed, laid the doll on the floor and lay down next to it. She said, "You know I use these dolls in my work. I get extra tips this way. I smear the man juices on a doll and he gives me more money. Now I stick pins into this doll and it gives me pleasure. I get my revenge." She laughed again, got off the floor and put the doll away.

I felt rather dumb about it. Not knowing how to respond I started to analyze her aggression.[1] I thought to myself how stupid and obvious can I be? I hope she doesn't see through this. She did. She got indignant and said that I was stupid. I agreed. She started to leave and I asked her for my fee. She turned and smiled and said, "Why man? What satisfaction have you given me?" I didn't respond. I began to doubt myself and the ability of my profession to deal with anything but mundane middle-class issues. I nodded my head as if I were about to answer my own question when I noticed something being slipped under the door. It looked like money. I walked over and picked up two pieces of a fifty dollar bill. I began to look for tape. I stopped dead in my tracks, took the money to the ashtray and burned it. I didn't know why nor did I care. I just wanted to get that woman out of my life. I began to berate myself and call myself superstitious.

On my way home I had a strange sense of self-contempt combined with a sense of awe—awe for her and contempt for

---

[1]Often rational explanations ensue when power fails. Every ivory tower needs an army to protect it.

myself. How boldly she lived. Every day was an adventure. Of course I had my adventures too—at least I thought so. I had my practice and a house to protect. She relied on her wits complete with demons, beauty and spirit. I relied on cleverness, belief in the system and the support of my colleagues who knew that psychotherapy[1] was superior to any other "mental healing system." I quickly consoled myself by thinking that her way and mine were just different.

When I got home I dealt with a few "emergencies." One patient had drunk too much and had thoughts of killing his wife. Another had an anxiety attack over a plane flight she was about to take. Another just wanted to tell me that she had her first orgasm while having intercourse. "Oh well," I said, "these are my adventures."

SEX OR INFORMATION

Three years passed before anything else happened along these lines. I was out of town having a drink at a classy hotel one evening. A fairly attractive black lady sat down on the stool next to me. She was a prostitute. She started to talk and I offered her a drink. I was sort of between marriages and thought—why not. I noticed that she had an accent. It sounded rather strange, like something I had heard before. I asked her a few questions that she readily answered. My mind flashed back to my patient and the "kitchen witch." I got excited and at the same time scared when I remembered the Voodoo dolls my patient carried. I looked to see if she had a big purse. When I saw that it was small I felt a sense of relief.

She began making her pitch. She had already asked me if I were I cop. Finally we agreed on a figure when a thought popped into my mind. "Instead of sex how about an interview. I'll pay her for information," I thought.

Then I remembered what one of my University professors said about data collected from prisoners and street people, "They

---

[1]Psychotherapy is now an institution. Like all good things, once accepted by the establishment it becomes a tool of the establishment. This is a real danger for occult groups—if they are accepted by society.

are so sensitive that they will do anything and say anything that will get them what they want." I let this thought slip away. I was excited by the prospect of having sex "intellectually."

We agreed to an hourly rate and I sensed that she had been paid to be "perverse" in this way before. However, she was shocked when I started talking about magic and prostitution.

She said, "What does a white man know of Voodoo?"

I said, "Very little, but I have studied Western magic."

"Well," she said, "I know little of what you speak, but mine is older."

"Yes, I know," I said. "I am interested in sex and magic and whether or not you and other prostitutes practice any kind of magic, whether for self-protection, good luck or revenge. I am also interested if you use sex to make your magic stronger."

"You want a lot for your money. But I won't talk here. Do you have a room?"

I said, "Yes," and anxiously took her there. I turned on the TV and made a couple of drinks. When I turned around she was lying on the bed looking very sexy. I began to have thoughts about sex. I guess she would have also preferred that. It would have been easier for her. But I was more excited about being a voyeur—peeking inside of her head—even if it was only listening to her lies.

She began, "Well, are you sure, honey that you would rather talk. I'm really good—you'll be surprised." I started to doubt myself again but persisted.

"Just talk and tell me things," I said.

"I was a young child when I left the Island, maybe five or six. I never knew my father. My mother and two sisters came to New York to live with my aunt. My older brothers stayed behind. My mother worked as a wash woman, doing clothes, cleaning up after the white man. I stayed at home with my older sisters. I went to school when I got older but never liked it."

I interrupted, "Tell me about Voodoo—or *Santeria* or...?"

"My religious tradition is older than yours—and yours doesn't even think that mine is a religion. Many of us have adopted yours to survive in your world. But it is not our world. We tolerate you—much as you need to look down on us. I'm a black woman—beautiful it is true—and like your ancestors you want

me. Then you took me—now you must pay. I'm not educ
like you—but I know more than you and your kind know. I
know from experience—from the streets—and from learning
how to tolerate humiliation. Like many of my sisters, I know
how to do this well.

"We have our own Gods and spirits. We do not worry about
an afterlife like you do—our religion is for living, for *now*. Our
religion is power—to give us what we want. You have fooled
yourself into thinking that you do not want power. You beg and
pray, but like me you want power. You have tricked yourself in
many ways. The white-man is a liar—a trickster—not only to
others but to himself. He wants to think well of himself. You and
your kind are deceivers—you are deceiving yourself right now
with me. I can read your mind—you're afraid of me sexually—
so you want to talk."

I replied, "Yes, in some ways I am fearful of being taken over
by you and I might add I also desire it. Much of what you say is
true but there are half-truths in what you say."

"It doesn't matter much," she replied, "your time is running
short and I want to give you something."

She opened her purse and gave me a drawing—more a
scribble—that I didn't recognize. It was the sigil of a spirit or
demon. I asked her what it meant and she replied that it was a
spirit that would help me conquer the fears of love. I thanked her
and asked for some more time. This time I didn't offer to pay.

She said, "If you pay more I'll stay." Secretly I was hoping
that she would stay for me. She knew that too because she
smiled.

"You hoped I would stay because I like you? I know these
things. I don't like you—you think too much of yourself—your
kind always does, no matter how kind and self-effacing you
appear—I know your kind. I do not have letters after my name—
I don't need them—you and your kind do. I have screwed lots of
your kind. I need to let them know how special they really are—
how really special—and how much I like and respect them—it is
easy to make your type jump. You feel so weak—you rely too
much on your weakest part. Your strength has been sapped.

"To tell you the truth I do use dolls with my men. I have taken
revenge on those of you who have harmed me. But dolls are

Hollywood. Voodoo, as you call it, does so much more. You are not a doer but a dabbler. You play, you don't believe because real Voodoo would terrify you. Your magic is weak—full of self-importance like your type is. Your type cheats on his wife and calls it something else. You think you have outwitted God. In Voodoo we become the spirit. We are taken over by God. We become one. You and your God live far from each other."

I interjected, "But I am not married now."

She replied, "You lie. You still love your last wife—you are married and you feel guilty even for this. You are scared being here alone with me. You feel you will lose your power with me. You would call this satisfying me, but it is really you that you are concerned with. But I am just a prostitute. I am not your mother or wife. In your mind they have to love you. All I have to do is screw you. But you are so concerned—you talk instead."

I looked at her with anger and respect. She began talking about possession.

"'Respectable' blacks want to disown Voodoo. Voodoo is their heritage—a black religion. But they prefer Christianity because it is the religion of their masters. Christianity is respectable—Voodoo is not. It is now only for the poor. Voodoo demeans those who wish to believe, they think. When a person is possessed the spirit takes over the body. The person is no longer himself. He or she is the spirit. He or she is someone else. This defiles your clean religion where you pray and listen to priests lecture you.

"Unlike Christianity and your science, Voodoo doesn't divorce spirit from matter. The world is still alive for us. For you it is dead."

We were both getting tired and I was becoming bored with her superiority. I politely dismissed her but not before thanking her. She sensed my insincerity and left.

After she was gone, I could still hear her voice in my head. It was as if I were possessed, not by my own ancestral spirits but by hers. I began to feel sorry that I didn't make love to her—I consoled myself with the thought that prostitutes don't make love with their clients.

By the time she left I had spent close to five hundred dollars and didn't even get laid. For a moment I felt like a fool—and then I laughed.

I can't say I learned anything new from her. I did gain a unique experience of a twentieth century prostitute who was still, psychologically speaking, living in a jungle.

THE MEGAPLEX—STRONG DESIRES & TIGHT SPACES

Living in a MegaPlex like Los Angeles can be quite challenging—in fact it can be quite terrifying. No longer a simple melting pot, the MegaPlex has become a pressure cooker.

People from various cultures, religions and races are thrown together in tight spaces and bombarded by high-tech info which both excites and horrifies them. Most of these people have escaped their own country to enjoy the freedom and prosperity of America. Most of these people, however, are quite surprised with what they find. One man who did occasional work for me told me, "It's better here, I send money home, I have five in the room maybe, I learn English, have a business of my own." Four years later he had his own cleaning and repair business. He cleaned, sanded and varnished boats. He was married and had two children. I thought to myself, how many of our children would be satisfied with that. I knew his next move—his first son would become a lawyer.

Within the brown mist of this concrete rain forest with flashing buildings and speeding cars, strong desires grow dark and ferment. What often emerges is horror for the white man— the original creator and inhabitant of this jungle. Now, like the American Indian, he is being displaced—his religion, values and economy are crumbling in the wake of high tech and brown colored people. He is retreating further and further into the forest, the hills and the desert—hoping beyond all hope to hold onto his mechanical way of life.

Yet, in alcoves throughout the MegaPlex there still lingers in hope and terror the remains of the middle-class while the wealthy are busy building higher fences and installing the latest security systems. The MegaPlex looks like an armed camp with gangs, drug dealers and street people littering the corners once occupied by well-dressed shoppers. The sale of guns and security systems have sky-rocketed and some neighborhoods look like prisons from the glut of wrought iron bars that face friend and foe alike.

Many intelligent inhabitants have sold their status symbols both to raise cash and to prevent their arms and fingers from being cut off. It's not smart to drive certain cars through certain areas. The driver might just be pulled out, and then beaten or killed while the culprit drives off. The cars are usually torn apart or shipped whole South of the Border or to the Far East.

This now is our civilization.

To combat these rapid and often terrifying changes, more and more laws are being created. In reality, these laws do not affect the street person, the gang member or, more importantly, the multitude of people who have so little to lose and so much to gain. These laws apply mostly to those who are already part of the culture—domesticated and made timid by ownership and their dependence on others to protect them. Success, particularly for the middle-class, has a high price—there is a lot to protect but not enough to get out and be free. So the answer is security, to retrench in their traditions while their world falls down around them.

As with all discomfort and pain, blame and a culprit are needed. It is normal to look for simple answers for unhappiness and fear, but it is also misleading and dangerous. There are so many potential individual and group culprits that it is convenient if the victim can find an underlying theme. In our culture, one common theme is Satanism.[1]

Satanism explains, for Raschke (in his book *Painted Black*) and so many others: rock music, mass murder, drugs, child abuse, addictions, Elvis, the disintegration of the family, skin heads, economic chaos, disobedience of children and much more. His definition of Satanism includes almost everything that doesn't appear to be blatant Christianity. (Jews are OK, of

---

[1]See *Painted Black*, Carl A. Raschke, Harper & Row, San Francisco: 1990. This book is full of references and arguments which prove little or nothing. However, the author does demonstrate how a good writing style, together with an active imagination and fear, combine to support the notion "whatever the believer believes, the prover proves."

course). Raschke's list includes alternative religions (in which the Occult is included), aspects of *Santeria*, Voodoo and the "infamous" OTO. We will look at the OTO because, unlike *Santeria* and Voodooism, it is a Western phenomena.

ALEISTER CROWLEY AND THE OTO

The authors—both members of the OTO—have met hundreds of Thelemites[1] including most of the OTO's leaders. To believe that the OTO is a major force in the promotion of Satanism is blatantly absurd. The majority of the members, while not leading ordinary lives, are quite normal in their beliefs and behavior. They may be defined as more mystical than magical, but not Satanic.

While some of the members may drink heavily and from time to time may have taken a few drugs, the Satanic accusation is completely false. Some members of the Order have described themselves simply as an "extended dysfunctional family." This last statement is usually said in jest.

Accusations and sensationalism prove nothing about the OTO's alleged Satanic affiliation. In fact, most members are appalled at the idea that the OTO is labeled Satanic. Even Anton LaVey is horrified that the OTO is called Satanic. He perceives this as an insult to his brand of Satanism.

While Aiwass, Crowley's "higher self," had Luciferian qualities, the OTO doesn't worship the Christian Satan. In some places in Crowley's writings, however, he does refer to Aiwass "as our master the Devil" and makes frequent references to Satan and the Devil.

In a footnote in Crowley's chapter on Black Magic[2] he gives us a taste of how he played with, and felt about, the Devil:

'The Devil' is, historically, the God of any people that one personally dislikes. This has led to so much

---

[1]A word used to describe those who belong to the religion of Thelema which was based on Crowley's *Book of the Law*. The OTO was the first Order to embrace the *Book of the Law*, but the some of the rituals practiced in the Order are older and come from a different origin.

[2]*Magick in Theory and Practice*, Aleister Crowley, Chapter XXI, pp. 190–205. Magickal Childe Publishing, New York: 1990.

> confusion that THE BEAST 666 has preferred to let names stand as they are, and to proclaim simply that AIWAZ—the solar-phallic-hermetic 'Lucifer' is his own Holy Guardian Angel, and "The Devil' SATAN or Hadit of our particular Starry Universe. This serpent, SATAN, is not the enemy of Man, but He who made Gods of our race, knowing Good and Evil; He bade 'Know Thyself!' and taught Initiation. He is the 'the Devil' of the Book of Thoth, and His emblem is BAPHOMET, the Androgyne who is the hieroglyph of arcane perfection...[1]

This is a fine opportunity to deal with this crucial issue. Satan, as we in the modern West understand him, is a Christian invention.

In the Old Testament he is simply the accuser. In the New Testament he is the incarnation of all the evil in the world. Some believe that Satan developed from the Greek character Dionysus, or Lucifer (the light bearer) in other eras. This makes some sense since Christianity regards Paganism (the old religion) as pure evil. Of course, Christianity regards everything as pure evil. We, however, regard Christianity as the greatest curse upon mankind.

Voodooism and magic are much older than Pan. Few scholars would disagree that magic and Voodooism are coextensive with the birth of man as we know him. If Africa is the Mother of our civilization, then Voodoo is the Mother of our religious impulse.

THE DEVIL MADE ME DO IT

Amid the horror[2] and chaos of Evil in the MegaPlex, a new breed of people are emerging. They are a mixture of the new and the old—of high tech and ancient beliefs. They program computers by day and perform magic at night. Some of them even practice Voodoo. Some of these practitioners have been brought up in the Voodoo tradition. Others are white and have adopted Voodoo, like magic, as their new religion. During the day they study physics and at night they practice Voodoo or, as some call it, black magic. We have called these people VoodooTechs. Others, however, call them Satanists.

---

[1]Ibid. p. 193.
[2]See Raschke's horror in *Painted Black*.

Raschke and his type *do* have something to be concerned about but it's not Satan. They are right when they fear the collapse of their civilization. It is collapsing, *but so what*. No doubt the ancient Greeks were horrified when they saw the signs of collapse. So were the Romans. And so were the Africans when they were invaded by the white.

We do not seem to realize that every changing or collapsing civilization sees their demise as evil. Every group sees their group as the pinnacle—the chosen—the best. In fact the Jews were so vocal about being the chosen people Hitler tried to destroy them because he saw his own people as the chosen ones.

The fact that the demise—or, more correctly, transmutation—of one civilization into another is associated with destruction should be of no surprise to Raschke or to anyone else. To believe that change is the result of evil is a sign that the believer has no sense of history or, for that matter, simple psychology.

One subtle effect of blaming is to regain an (illusory) sense of power in the face of failure. We see how quickly we search for someone to blame when something goes wrong. It is not simply to find out the facts but to regain the sense of power lost by failure. The name of "devil" is not given only to another God—it is given to his followers as well.

CAN WE GET OUT BEFORE WE HIT BOTTOM?

One major sign of a declining culture—and for that matter a declining human being—is the inability to recognize what is to its advantage. You can experience this for yourself by visiting a so-called retirement home. In theory people are placed there because they are unable to care for themselves. But it seems that more and more people are falling into this group without the benefit of twenty-four hour care. They are the decaying and horrified middle-class.

In the face of the collapse of the old civilization it is not surprising that Christians have regressed to a "spiritual" but more violent form of their religion. (I, for one, would argue about their spiritual qualities, as their "religious zeal" seems to fester more with dogma and hate than spirit.) In this sense the new Christian is a happy man. He sees every change, every event, as a sign of the second Coming and the destruction of his

*hristian religion requires chaos, violence and
o prove itself legitimate.* Without Satan,
ath and destruction the entire religion becomes a
, destruction and change occur independent of
it is the nature of mankind to undergo change.

A similar return to orthodoxy has happen among Jews as well. The popularity of Halachic Judaism and the mystical Jewish tradition symbolizes a need for "the return" and the finding of roots. After the failed rebellion of the 1960s, many people are searching for their roots.

As the old Roman Church dies, the last vestige of the spiritual in Christianity also goes. This is particularly destructive for the middle-class—the heirs of the worst of materialism and religion.

It is by this group of people—their children especially—that more foreign religions are being adopted. This was once particularly true for the religions of the East—Buddhism and Hinduism—and now the religion is Voodoo.

A new quality comes from the special combination of the organic religion—Voodoo—and high technology—computers. This marriage—predicted thirty-five years ago by the futurist Marshall McLuhan—is not a marriage free from difficulties.

The modern world doesn't hold out the opportunities it did just a few years ago. Many young people, particularly of the middle and upper-middle-class, are "late bloomers" who spend more time with their parents—unemployed and single.

The ability to own a home, to make a fast dollar, has taken a back seat—for simpler things and finding "meaning" in life. In their search for meaning and with additional time on their hands they have begun to dabble not with the toys of the wealthy, as their parents did, but with the toys of the poor. They realized that their parents' attempts to imitate the wealthy and powerful only trapped them deeper into slavery. In other words it was much easier to become "middle-class" than to become really powerful. The social ladder doesn't have equal steps no matter what freshman sociology teaches.

It may be only coincidence or it may be a fact of life that the disinherited and disenfranchised are the ones who keep tradition alive. I am speaking of the slaves from Africa who, in the face of a real Christian hell (capture and slavery), kept their heritage alive. Our modern youth, who feel like those who lost their homeland—their dreams—are looking for substance, something that will give them power. Many feel hostile toward the older generation who, they feel, have stolen their dreams through greed, deceit and hypocrisy.

Technology and money didn't set their parents free; it enslaved them in more devious ways.

Living inside a computer screen, although entertaining, can't take the place of the feeling of "living" power. The practice of Voodoo is very active—commanding spirits, pronouncing strange names, weird sounds, smells, dancing and the killing of animals. This creates a real feeling of power and, sometimes, horror. For most of us real adventure is gone. We live in our chairs. Modern man is cut off from the organic roots of the hunt—of exploring the unknown.

Voodoo and computers operated by the same person may sound strange but it isn't. The spirits of the screen and the spirits of the dead—both are "doing things" behind the scenes. Who ever sees a computer work? More people have seen spirits than have seen a computer operate from the inside out. They know the lingo but do they really understand what happens inside? Computers and spirits are like consciousness—we see the results but don't really experience what goes on behind the scenes.

When civilization collapses there are no odd bedfellows. Latino and black and oriental and white. Children of colors—a genetic soup. This to the horror of the dying, whose belief in their tradition (myth) gave them a perch from which to find order in the world. No—their order is almost gone. Not only are the taboos against inter-faith and inter-class and inter-sex and inter-heritage dying, but now the death of the inter-race taboo. Where will the desecration end? Could it be with the end of death itself—the very death which the Christian fascists worship?

Now the "children" are into Satanism, Voodoo, magic, Wicca and high-tech. "New" symbols mean anxiety but to say that this is an age of anxiety would be to understate the case. No—it's not an age of anxiety but an age of *terror*. Though some of the old restrictions are gone this is still not a time to rejoice. At least we knew who they were. Now the enemy is ourselves. Our very life is becoming an auto-immune deficiency disease. We are developing deadly allergies.

What is before us is an new war—an inter-generational war.

Recently I was invited to what a traditional Voodooist would consider a benign religious celebration. A group of people were standing around chanting and watching a couple have "religious sex." This was a ritual, a magical-religious experience, complete with symbols and a "priest."

People drank sacramental wine and ate sacramental cakes. While some people might find sex and religion odd bedfellows, for this group there was no difference. Sex was religion and religion was sex. Most of these people were computer literate and many had high-tech jobs. They were dissatisfied with the "traditional" religious rituals and sought out strange and unusual practices to satisfy their religious longings.

While all of this strangeness is going on there is another new religious experience emerging. It is Fundamentalism with a big *F* and it does not characterize itself as inherently Christian. This secular religion holds that whatever was of value forty years ago is the *Truth*. Its priests are detectives of the soul who believe that all sorts of things are wrong everywhere and with everybody. This secular religion is called "psychotherapy." An example of this is the recent attempt by some psychotherapists to reduce demonic possession to a psychiatric diagnosis.[1]

Regarding possession as a pathology can severely limit the effectiveness of Western healers when dealing with people who have different belief systems. One with a different belief system is put under the control of someone who demands that he or she give up those beliefs or be considered insane. This can be especially stressful if the practitioner has the power to institutionalize the patient—merely because of differing beliefs.

---

[1]Psychopathological states have been reduced to a numerical reference system. These have been organized and published as the Diagnostic Statistical Manual (DSM). Some psychologists and psychiatrists want to create a Psychopathological category for possession—named, of all things—Possessive States Disorder. The DSM helps professionals communicate with each other and makes it possible for them to collect from insurance carriers. Unfortunately, they have, like most of us, confused communication with truth.

This attitude removes any hope of psychotherapy's ever having the status as a scientific treatment and moves it closer to where it belongs—religion. As a religion its bigotry and intolerance for other religions (healing models) can be better understood.

Another similar religious quality of the new psychotherapy is its pre-occupation with abuse and addiction—the new sins. Everyone is believed to be in a state of denial concerning being abused and abusing others. Any strong interest is held up to scrutiny as it may be hiding a secret addiction. Like the witch hunts of old the new psychotherapy assumes a set of symptoms and diseases and then finds them. If they can't be found the person is obviously hiding (denying) them. This "thinking" is no different than original sin. It suffers from the inability to question assumptions or even recognize the existence of assumptions.

This return to "fundamentals" takes place during periods of weakness or burnout before new and powerful energies emerge. Yet, the ignorance of this movement is matched by few other experiences in my life. What a horror if it were true that this "fundamentalism" is an advancement in science like most of these people believe.

One of their key concepts is "boundaries" but their demarcation points are strangely narrow and conventional. They perceive Voodoo as madness and rightfully so from their point of view—for they are the mental health experts.

Few of them have ever stopped to think that mental illness is just as invisible as spirits. Yet, armed with words, they prowl—looking for demons they can dress-up with nomenclature. For these "men and women of science" Voodooism may be nothing but hypnosis. These seekers of truth should remember that hypnosis is not a well-anchored concept. Its boundaries are fuzzy. And if demon possession is "nothing but hypnosis" then why isn't belief in God "nothing but hypnosis." Some may agree with this, but there is something more sinister about Voodoo. And what may this be? The refusal to relinquish the body for the mind. The willingness to live with a complex set of continua rather than either/or dualism.

Recently I read an article by a Latino mental health expert who believes that *Santeria* fosters dependency upon the *Santero* and that this is "bad." This assertion borders on the ridiculous since every competent *Santero* provides his client with self-treatment remedies to strengthen the client's spiritual protection. Did the "mental health expert" ever question what *his* profession fosters? Not just dependency upon the therapist, but dependency upon consensus as well.

A number of months later I read a response to this article in the same "journal" applauding the "expert's" view. The gentleman who wrote this response was a psychotherapist who also held an advanced degree "in the ministry."

I see very little difference between psychotherapy and Voodoo in terms of its effectiveness. Psychotherapists, of course, hide behind a government issued license to practice. This provides value and power (status) for the practitioner—but not necessarily for the patient, particularly if he or she is from a culture which holds beliefs which conflict with the ideology and institutions of the host[1] environment.

Most scientific psychologists call psychotherapy "mumbo-jumbo." Some even call it Voodoo.

Now let's get to the point. The entire issue here is one of power. Everyone wants power—their place in the sun. So far so good, but to wage war against the competition and call one's own treatment science, as many psychotherapists do, or morality as the Christians do—well, these are signs of people whose sense of power is weakening. They are easily threatened by the competition and they lack any sense of intellectual integrity.[2]

---

[1]While all analogies break down sooner or later, playing with analogies can be fun. The host culture almost always attacks foreign material by destroying it, segregating it or assimilating it. This, of course, is what appeared to happen to African religions in the New World. However, one method of resistance is to take on the identity of the host while maintaining one's self in secret. The pantheon of Catholic Saints gave the slaves the opportunity to accomplish this *tour de force*.

[2]In all fairness, when I did a literature search on Voodoo and *Santeria* there were a number of excellent articles describing the effectiveness of both as a treatment modality for believers. Some researchers even suggest that Western intervention be combined with more traditional forms of treatment. One researcher cautioned, however, that any form

While not all psychotherapists are against the use of foreign methods of treatment, most conceptualize the patient who believes in Voodoo as suffering from psychological problems. I doubt very seriously that a person who feels possessed by an evil spirit sees himself as having a psychological problem. Instead, he sees himself as being possessed by a demon.

Although a bit different, the next example will help convey how researchers and scholars miss the point—they demand that what they observe "mean" to everyone else what it means to them.

The use of the Christian cross in Voodoo ceremonies has frequently been interpreted to mean that the cross reflects the deep influence of Christianity on Voodoo. There is no doubt that the practitioners of Voodoo correlated the pantheon of Christian saints with their own African spirits. Thus present day forms of Voodoo are an amalgam of various traditions. But the presence of outside influences in no way makes Voodoo less of a religion in its own right.

Unfortunately, for the sleeping habits of these scholars who are horrified that Voodoo is a legitimate religion, the cross is an ancient symbol used by Africans in their homeland to represent the crossroads where matter and spirit meet. The cross represents the point where the sacred meets the profane. The cross also represents the cosmos and the four quarters of the universe where the various deities reside.

The role of Christianity—and even Islam—in modern day Voodoo, *Santeria* and *Yoruba* is a simple function of historical development. These alien religions have been incorporated into the African religions as a result of cultural influences, particularly slavery and colonization.

Recently some African-Americans have suggested that the term *Santeria* be de-emphasized and the *Yoruba* religion substituted. This is a result of a desire to emphasize the basic roots of *Santeria*—African. While there are significant differences between the original African religions and what we have today, the desire to emphasize African origins is understandable. However, we believe that this movement will not take hold in

---

of Western intervention should be very short in duration and that the practitioner should adopt an "authoritarian" posture.

ιallest communities since an overwhelming
teria participants are Cuban, Puerto Rican,

ιolars like Dr. Neeley,[1] believe that "Voodooism
ιll Afro-American religions" regardless of *who* is
practicing it. We believe that this also applies to whites who
have strong leanings toward Voodoo but who, in our Christian
world, are labeled as black magicians.

Neeley feels that the attempt by white "clerics" to destroy
African religion failed. Voodoo, by whatever name, signifies
Africa and its retention in the Western world was achieved by
holding on to the songs, magic, healing methods, dances, rituals
and language of the original religion.

Voodoo has often been regarded as an expression of the racial
and cultural resistance of an oppressed class of people within a
hostile society.

The term "Diaspora" is often associated with the Jewish
people who were scattered throughout the world, yet many Jews
retained the practices of their original religion even if it meant
their death.

However, most Jews were assimilated into their new culture.
Few whites think of the enslavement of the Africans as similar.
The term "African Diaspora" is rarely seen except in literature
written by Africans.

The re-emergence of Voodoo in the United States is similar to
the re-emergence of the "return" of many Jews to their ancestral
religion. What is meant by "ancestral religion" is the Orthodox
practice of Judaism and not its Christianized version as practiced
by most Jews in the United States.

It is ironic and horrifying that most Americanized Jews are
taught to believe in Christian values while still being discrim-
inated against as Jews. No matter how hard the Jews have tried
to emulate their Christian oppressors, they are still regarded as
strange and looked upon suspiciously. Little jokes are still made

---

[1]*Contemporary Afro-American Voodooism (Black Religion): The
Retention and Adaptation of the Ancient African-Egyptian Mystery
System.* Bobby Joe Neeley, University of California, Berkeley,
Dissertation Abstracts, p. 1100, 1988.

and snide comments applied. While it is not regarded as "in," Jews are thought of as Christ killers and "aliens." Sometimes they are referred to as "white niggers." (The Catholics, of course, have "forgiven" the Jews for killing their God.) Jews are taught Christian ethics and morality and psychologically feel more guilt for violating facets of the Christian religion than of their own.

Similarly the Africans were taught Christianity, but unlike the Jews they were not allowed to have temples of their own. The African religion become publicly annihilated. Most African-Americans today practice Christianity and have given up their heritage for the promise of a middle-class life. However, some African-Americans didn't. They retained and practiced their original religion in secret and in today's environment are returning to their own religion. Like the Jew, African-Americans were not allowed to practice their religion in its original form. Jews and African-Americans are not publicly allowed multiple wives nor are they allowed to practice animal sacrifice. Recently, however, the Supreme Court of the United States decriminalized animal sacrifice for religious purposes, but still some local authorities continue their harassment. Still, regardless of how the court ruled, the spirit of animal sacrifice and the practice of African religion is gone for most African-Americans. They, like many Jews, have adopted the religion which enslaved, humiliated and tortured them. Christianity is the unofficial "official" religion of the United States regardless of guarantees promised by the Constitution and the Bill of Rights.

In today's world, African-Americans are beginning to move out of the back rooms of store fronts and open temples of worship of their own. Here they chant and play drums, perform rituals and invoke spirits. However, we as whites have not observed or have not been allowed to observe the practice of animal sacrifice.

Yet, the practice of the blood sacrifice goes on both in the world of *Santeria* and in the world of *Yoruba*. The emphasis on the blood sacrifice horrifies the white middle-class. For some of them this represents the return to barbarism and to others it represents the practice of Satanism. From a sociological point of view, however, it may simply mean the end of a particular way of life.

It is a major error to believe that Voodoo is simply the religion of the poor. This is no doubt due to prejudice and the constant media influence concerning certain Caribbean countries and Latino nations. However, we shouldn't be deluded by this form of propaganda.

The facts remain otherwise. Over the past few years I have met more and more people who are practicing Voodoo. For example, I met one educated thirty year old white female who used Voodoo rituals to get even with her boyfriend. If her parents knew that their upper-middle-class Christian-raised daughter had performed a Voodoo ritual (which included the sacrifice of a number of insects) they might have died of shame and horror. This is but one example of middle-class, educated white folk practicing Voodoo to gain what they want or to take revenge. Surely, this is not the Christian way.

The sacrifice of animals, chanting, invoking the names of foreign Gods, dancing and singing are not the only forms of "black" magic being practiced. While the media focuses much of its hysteria on such things as the painting of upside-down pentagrams or some nut's killing a bunch of people and claiming that "Satan made him do it," more and more normal people are practicing sex magic. They embark on this practice for a number of reasons, some of which border on the ridiculous—from a rational point of view. For example, some will use the sexual fluids for charging a gold or silver ring to attract wealth. Others use the sexual act as a sacrifice to gain riches, take revenge, gain a lover or simply to spiritualize the sexual experience. These rituals, as well as many others, are not practiced just by the poor and uneducated, but also by the educated and the wealthy. The media doesn't report this. Could it be due to lack of knowledge, or, maybe, because they are too embarrassed or—who knows— perhaps it hits too close to home.

There may be some hope for those who feel that the "foreign religions" taking over America will not find a soil free from internal conflicts. Some scholars believe that there will be significant changes in *Santeria* due to the use of the African name *Yoruba*. Some wonder if the name change might result in a change of identity. And other conflicts may arise from the power politics between African-Americans and Latinos.

Most scholars do not believe that any significant changes in ritual practices will occur. The changes associated with the name *Yoruba* may be more significant than immediately meets the eye as more African-Americans become directly involved with their own religion and leave the "white religion" of Christianity.

The effort to destigmatize the original African Religion has yet to meet strong resistance from the community at large. However, this may change as more whites embrace Voodoo and further erode the monopoly which Christianity holds on American religious values and behavior.

It will be very difficult for Christian-American parents to imagine their children involved with African dress, animal sacrifice, spirit invocation, African sexual rituals and trance experiences.

Unlike the hypocrisy taught by Christianity, the *Yoruba* religious culture doesn't split the spiritual from the practical and this quality of Voodoo, in itself, holds a larger seed of destruction for America's "native" religion than anything else.

The major concern for the white community at large will be the fear that there will be more erosion of middle-class values as African religions spread throughout the community. This may lead to a new group of victims—those who practice alternative religions to Christianity. Groups like the Ku Klux Klan and the Aryan Nation may find further grist for their mill of hatred as Voodoo begins to permeate the life of whites.

Satan will again become the scapegoat for the diminishing power and value of God's Chosen People—White Christian Americans. This is particularly ironic since it was the superior white race that enslaved the African. Now African religion is taking "revenge."

Historically there appears to be a strong association between the embracing of foreign religions and cultural disintegration. More people may find themselves polarized and looking for sanctuary as the cities become more possessed by alien religions—particularly with the participation of white youth. Religious purity will join with racial purity as a slogan.

CHAPTER EIGHT

CHRISTIANITY, VOODOO & DIONYSUS

Christopher S. Hyatt, Ph.D.

> *Gods of Hellas, gods of Hellas,*
> *Can ye listen in your silence?*
> *Can your mystic voices tell us*
> *Where ye hide? In floating islands,*
> *With a wind that evermore*
> *Keeps you out of sight of shore?*
> *Pan, Pan is dead.*[1]
> E.B. Browning, *The Dead Pan*

We ultimately know the soul and spirit of a man by the way he defines his relationship to The Numinous. To say this differently, we know the strength of a man by the way he lives his life in relation to his idea of God. These assertions rest on the assumption that The Numinous, the unknown, God(s) is a primary need, not simply for protection, or for utilitarian needs, nor, simply for "meaning" but for the "feeling of life" itself. Without The Numinous—"the wild card"—life loses its enchantment.

If everything in the Universe could be known and controlled, man would no longer exist as we know him. Thus, to know the nature of a man we must ask how he defines The Numinous for himself and *how he lives* The Numinous in his life. Thus, the

---

[1]Pan never died. It is ironic that Panism is rearing its head again in the Citadel which claimed to replace it—the modern Christian City.

God(s) of every culture, like the God(s) of every man, are a sign of its strength or weakness—its joys and pains.

In this chapter we examine three types of Gods. The God of the Christian, the Gods of Africa and a God of the early Greeks—Dionysus.

An example, using a number of seven point scales, may give us some deeper insight.

Rate the Christian God:

Strong	— — — — — — —	Weak	**Doesn't apply
Orderly	— — — — — — —	Chaotic	**Doesn't apply
Lustful	— — — — — — —	Chaste	**Doesn't apply

Now ask yourself is this God primarily, forgiving, vengeful or "indifferent." Choose one.

Now rate the image of mankind as each particular God defines him.

Strong	— — — — — — —	Weak	**Doesn't apply
Orderly	— — — — — — —	Chaotic	**Doesn't apply
Lustful	— — — — — — —	Chaste	**Doesn't apply

Do this for your image of the "African Gods."

Do this for Dionysus.

For the fun of it, and for a better sense of how this system works, do this for Buddha and for the Jewish God.

This comparative method provides a map of how a culture or a man conceives of himself in relationship to The Numinous.

Before we travel further on this adventure we must be prepared. We often hear that human decency emerged from Christianity and that it may disappear with its death[1]. Some even

---

[1]Since Christianity developed later than Greek philosophy and Voodooism, it is often regarded as superior to both. This reasoning is based on the assumption of progress: everything that follows something is superior to what preceded it. This fallacy rests on the illusion that 'developmental' means 'superior.'

Another error is based on Darwin's notion of 'fitness.' It is believed that only the fittest survive. Besides being a tautology, this assertion is not provable, and is based on the assumption that the future is always 'better' than the past. It is also based on the belief the 'higher' evolves from the 'lower.' Each species is a species in itself. We are not 'better'

believe that modern civilization sprang from the head of Christianity and that the decay of this Civilization is the direct result of the weakening of Christianity's hold over mankind.

On the other hand Satan, Lucifer, and the Devil are indecent and in the service of the Anti-Christ incarnate. Of course, the Jews and just about everyone else have been included in the indecent group. This includes the Protestants who in turn regard the Pope as the Devil.

Dirt, darkness, hair, the sex organs, and, for that matter, anything to do with the body is indecent and belongs to the realm of the Devil.

One can see the associations that the early slavers had to the Africans and their religion and how easy it would be for them to associate both to Satan and the Devil.

Voodooism was a sign of a demonic race and had to be bred out of the slaves by torture. Although the Africans could not practice their religion publicly, they continued in darkness. It is ironic that the African Gods are taking revenge on the white man—as are the religions of the American Indians which are "stealing" disciples away from the Christians with Shamanism.

It is also interesting to recall that Christians considered Rock and Roll to be the work of the Devil and a direct influence of the African culture.

In much of the Western world, Christianity has been so successful that, no matter what you call yourself, you are still obliged to follow the laws of Christianity. Decency, from this point of view, was always followed by the sword. Recently I watched a television program which claimed to symbolize world peace. A band played "Onward Christian Soldiers." Apparently they had no idea what they were doing. The important point to keep in mind is that Christianity has nothing to do with God and nothing to with "decency." In fact Christianity's main purpose is to take over the world and make it it's slave. There are few other religions in the world which concern themselves so much with conversions.

---

than dogs or fishes. We are *different*. All of these errors are based on a further assumption; that there is one absolute starting point and one absolute ending point. A circular or spiral notion of time would lead to totally different conclusions.

People concerned with decency often think of themselves as moralists, or humanists. Anyone who dares think a little knows that human decency has nothing to do with Christianity. To the contrary, Christianity was one of first religions to take revenge upon the entire world—on life itself. It did this by teaching that man and the world were fundamentally evil. It taught that the body was nothing compared to the soul. Christianity had proof for its assertion. And what was this proof? That there was misery and pain in the world. This fact didn't prove the verdict of guilt which the judge—Paul—pronounced against the world. What it did demonstrate was the nature and character of the judge himself.

Buddha, for example, saw the same misery, but did not pronounce the world and mankind evil. His solution was more sound—treat the disease.

This is the difference between approaching something from a practical point of view with a semblance of strength and dignity and from approaching the same problem from the vile and dirty mind of a failure. Who is more decent? Who is more gracious? Who is more generous?

THE FIRST CHRISTIAN'S REVENGE AGAINST LIFE

Revenge is defined thusly: "To impose or inflict injury in return for injury or insult." What was the injury or insult life first inflicted on Paul for such hatred to brew? Naturally, Paul's birth and Paul's weakness. And how did Paul take his revenge? By teaching men to hate their body and their mind. He also vehemently hated women.

What men did he teach? Those who felt weak. Those who didn't belong to the elite, except those who saw a wonderful opportunity to gain a sickly type of power. He taught hate and revenge to the outcasts, the criminals, the cowards and to those who felt too weak to live with death. And they listened.

He promised a new world—another world after this one— where the chosen could sit next to God and watch their enemies suffer. What did Paul really teach? Revenge in the afterlife—in exchange for obedience in this life.

THE MAGIC OF FAITH

For many the real horror associated with the destruction of the Christian religion is the loss of heaven and immortality. The fear of losing heaven and eternal life is understandable—for to dwell on the permanency of death is horrifying for most of us.

Even more horrifying is the fear of eternal torture in hell. Much of this fear is predicated on Christian cosmology which creates a chasm between man and his God. This chasm is mediated by priests. In this sense man feels alone and isolated from his God.[1] Feeling alone and isolated requires action and, whether this action is morbid dependency or violence against perceived enemies, the result is the same—emptiness.

The notion of absolute good and evil also contributes to fear. There is one Good God and the Evil One. The ancient Greeks didn't have this split. Life was complex and so were the Gods. Each could do evil as well as good. Not only were the Gods capable of anything, they were immediate—they were alive among men. Sometimes they were friendly and at other times they were sadistic.

The Greek point of view was more in accord with reality. Life was a continuum, not a set of discrete categories. Monotheism, however, particularly in the Christian sense demands not only *one* God but an *isolated* God. The problem of evil for the monotheist is a complicated one "solved" finally by faith and belief—in metaphysical drivel.

Monotheism not only demands one isolated God, but one type of spirit as well: "equal in the eyes of God." The Greek mind didn't see its Gods as equal to each other, nor did it view people that way. With a multitude of Gods there was a multitude of spirits. People were different. There were types: the philosopher, the warrior, the merchant, the tiller of soil, ugly people, beautiful people, nobles and slaves. While mobility among these groups was possible, it required exceptional acts and abilities.

---

[1]Much of Christian cosmology is based on a the idea of an absolute starting point and a absolute ending point. A linear notion of time allows for convenient separations and absolute discrete categories, such as Heaven and Hell—Good and Bad. This type of thinking can best be described as Either/Or.

Christian religion solved the problem (at least in fantasy) of inequality (God's creations) by reducing all standards to the lowest common denominator. Thus, everyone is told that hard work and persistence are enough to gain stature and property in the community. While this is true up to a point, it is not enough and can never be enough. The communists have realized this—they tried but couldn't create a Christian heaven on earth by reducing life to its lowest common denominator—the worker.

OVERFLOWING WITH JOY

When I feel full of the feeling of joy, people tend to perceive me as kind. I am overflowing with myself and I desire to express this. I will even do things for people I normally loathe. Often this is experienced as kindness by others. This idea of overflowing is similar to the idea of the radiating creative energy of God which many mystics embrace. Sometimes this overflowing is seen as harmful in terms of another's experience—for example, a person may feel small because he can't return a gift in kind—but this implies nothing about the nature of the act of overflowing with energy and joy. The idea of overflowing with life and energy is much closer to the magical point of view expressed in a Voodoo ceremony. On the other hand Christian ritual and ceremony are clearly defined by restriction, by a lack of overflowing. They are stiff, implying a holding back. This is in direct contradiction to the idea of God itself, who created the world from desire and creative energy which flowed from his Primal nature. God, from this point of view, is a never-ceasing burst of light and power. He is forever brilliant as he flows outward and receives back his eternal Power. Mystical visions such as these are antithetical to the meek and the mild and to the form of worship performed by modern day Christians. Voodoo rituals on the other hand are closer to the mystical view

Sometimes I act kindly when I am fearful—that is, I hope to avoid some misfortune. Sometimes I have other motivations. Regardless of my reason, I am perceived as kind, and kindness is something almost everyone desires.

I shall provide a few examples of people who invoked the concept of "decency" when what they wanted was revenge.

Case 1

An associate of mine invested some money with a broker who said he could earn a seventeen percent return on his investment. At that time, most other people were only getting eight percent.

Being greedy and feeling very deserving—something which this person enjoys denying about himself—he leaped at the opportunity. Reality was suspended, much like a suicide victim's thoughts about gravity on the way down from the 30th floor.

He invested his money, received two or three payments and then received nothing more. He was very depressed and disturbed, complaining that his judgment about others was poor. I smiled and agreed, but added that his judgment about himself was even worse. He angrily responded that the broker was licensed, had a family and beautiful offices. He said that the man lacked "human decency."

In this context "decency" didn't mean kindness, but meant obligation. The broker was obligated to repay my associate for his own greed and ignorance. He trusted him and was disappointed. Here we tease out the meaning. He believed that his own greed, coupled with his sense of uniqueness, would suspend reality—but it didn't.

Reality emerged—and with disappointment came anger—with anger came revenge—when revenge was frustrated came weakness and impotency—with impotency came more moralizing—followed by depression, self-flagellation and more anger. He began to discuss notions of karma and other more abstract forms of punishment—his potency began to return. I watched with amazement—I began to feel superior until I remembered how I had done similar things.

The point which we must note is that morality takes the place of power. And that the essence of this morality is impotency and revenge.

A similar thing happened to another associate of mine. This time I suggested that we do a "spell" to cause his enemy harm.

Case 2

At first he felt excited about it—then claimed that it was wrong. When I pushed him further he admitted that he was frightened— that he would suffer more from doing harm to his enemy. I asked him how he would suffer. He replied that whatever he wished on his enemies would come back on him. (It is amazing how hedonistic moralists are.)

Finally, he challenged me that it wouldn't work anyway. I told him that it might, and anyway, what did he have to lose—at worst it would give him a feeling of power for an hour or so.

I suggested that the spell could be seen as medicinal—therapeutic—cathartic. He agreed, but as we began he became frightened. "For something that couldn't work why should you be scared," I said. He stated that it was wrong and that he would feel better if we stopped. I agreed to stop but told him that I would proceed with the ritual alone later. He was annoyed but didn't tell me not to do the ritual.

What we have here is a Ph.D. who tacitly believes in magic but denies it, moralizes about violence because he is scared he will be punished in an afterlife (which he denies believing in) and then allows me to do the ritual, so if his enemy is hurt he can enjoy it but it will be my fault. Clever fellow! This is the essence of modern man.

I performed the spell for my associate as an experiment. I hoped that he would ask me something about it. He didn't—for years. One day he called me and informed me that his enemy had been seriously injured in a car accident. I anxiously waited for him to ask me about the spell—but he didn't. Instead he stated that he felt sorry for his enemy—and felt bad that he had thought such terrible things about him. I couldn't help myself—I confessed. There was silence on the phone followed by—"that's on your head—not mine."

We continued talking for a few moments and then ended the conversation. We met for lunch two months later. He informed me that his now ex-enemy was back on his feet but suffered from chronic back pain. I asked him if he was glad. He said "no." My associate is a decent person.

Revenge: "To impose or inflict injury in return for injury or insult." My associate had all the reasons in the world to harm his enemy. But, he didn't. He didn't even proceed legally—it would have cost him too much money and embarrassment. Yet, my associate had convinced himself that his refusal to take revenge was based on his moral beliefs. He could now feel superior as well as safe.

Shall we reward a man and call it virtue because he didn't strike back out of fear? Or shall we call it a virtue when a man can strike back with impunity and doesn't? Who is the Christian? Who is more virtuous? Who is the powerful?

(Jason Black intrudes:

Regarding the above comment by Hyatt's friend that it was on *his* head, that is emphatically untrue in most traditional magical or religious systems. In fact, in any of the Afro-Caribbean traditions it is always explicitly understood that the person making the request is morally responsible for the spell. The hands of the magician are clean. He cannot, after all, know if the curse he is about to throw is "justified" or not, and must rely on the word of the client. All the nonsense about "karma" and "rebounding spells" that you see in modern occult literature is a seedy holdover from the last century and the influence of Theosophy. It has nothing to do with tradition or real psychic experience.

Regarding this man's self-contradictory attitude toward magic, I have two similar stories to tell:

A couple of years ago, I was sitting in a neighborhood bar. Someone I had never seen before sat down beside me, apparently in the mood to talk. He said he was a lighting technician for concert tours and this sparked my interest since I used to do that sort of thing myself. After we talked for a while somehow I began talking about trance phenomena in Haiti. His first response was a derisive bark of laughter. He insisted that it was all faked. I told him about the many instances of disbelieving strangers (like himself) who were spontaneously possessed, spoke in languages they did not know and performed psychic feats such as handling fire. When he asked how such things could be, I began to talk about quantum theory. Rather to my surprise, he knew all about this, and reluctantly agreed that modern theoretical physics *did* allow for magic.

Here is where things got strange. He was a little tipsy by this time and his defenses were coming down. He began to tell me a story. When he was much younger he worked as a chef in a good restaurant, and he had his own (expensive) set of knives. One day a particularly nice (and expensive) piece turned up missing. He believed he knew who had taken it and was enraged. The culprit came in to work and gave him sly little smiles throughout the day, driving him to new heights of anger. At one point he was cutting meat and thinking about the theft when he stabbed violently at the meat while envisioning the thief. At that moment, he heard a scream from across the kitchen and looked up to see his nemesis bent over, holding his arm which was drenched in blood. At the moment of his vision, the other man, who was also cutting something, severed one of his fingers and had to be rushed to the hospital to have it reattached. When the man returned to work, he walked up to my acquaintance, returned the knife without a word, and never spoke to him again. Both men "knew" who was responsible for the injury.

I was flabbergasted. The rational materialist was actually hiding a fear of the evil eye. By the time I left he was begging me almost in tears not to practice "black magic."

My second story regards a simple tarot reading I did for a friend many years ago. He wanted to know if his relationship with his girlfriend would continue or not. The cards said quite flatly, not. This ultimately turned out to be the case. A mutual friend was present at the reading. He said he didn't believe any of it but would apologize to me if the reading came true. As I said, it did, but apologize he did not. I later discovered that this "rationalist" spread the story that I had cursed the relationship and caused the entire series of events myself. This story was subsequently spread to many of my friends. Thus I was transformed by the rationalist from a gullible crank into a being of sinister and godlike power in one fell swoop. He has made no effort, then or ever, to discuss the matter with me.

It was not the last time I had such an experience. I suppose I'm lucky none of the local milk went sour.

I return you to Dr. Hyatt.)

One of the first things you learn in journalism is to ask and have answers for the following questions: who, what, where, why, when, and how. This method is ideal for finding out what is missing in any story as well as in any argument.

Ask first—who is talking, what is he saying, "can it be tied down to something factual," where is this taking place, why is he talking, when is he talking and how is he talking. Now ask, when does a person run for cover? Where does he sneak in assertions? When does he become metaphysical? How metaphysical does he become?

The Christian simply asserts and then "proves" by more assertions, appeals and fear.

THE EXPERIMENTAL RELIGIONIST

How do the assertions of the Christian differ from the Voodooist who also believes in God as well as spirits? I will first answer *why I* prefer Voodoo over Christianity. First, it's exciting—it's alive. Second, it's fun. Third, it interests me. Fourth, I feel power. Fifth, I have seen and experienced *some* results which could not be explained by simple psychology or faith.

When I tried Christianity, the only thing I felt was temporary relief from fear, some pleasurable fantasies, a sense of superiority over those who didn't practice, a sense of belonging to a larger community and, finally, boredom. I also had more friends.

The practice of Christianity was difficult to give up. It was easy to believe. Being a Christian had many rewards during times of crisis. Relief required little action on my part. I could be both lazy and fearful and still feel better.

Christianity was useful to me. However, usefulness does not make something true. The concept "truth" can't be applied to what can't be *disproved.* Nor does pleasure or pain make something true. Similar statements can be made about Voodoo.

For the reader's information, I have also experimented with being a Jew, a Nazi, a Buddhist, a Thelemite, a Golden Dawn enthusiast, a rationalist, a communist, an existentialist, an atheist, a democrat, a republican, a materialist, a psychotherapist, etc.

One similarity between the Voodooist and the Christian is, of course, the pantheon of spirits. Note, however, that many slaves were able to match up Christian Saints with Voodoo spirits, but the similarity stops there. However, a similar statement can be made regarding the pantheon of Greek Gods and Voodoo spirits.

Voodooists, however, actively use the spirits for both "good and evil" purposes—often the same spirit can do both good and evil. While a Christian may pray to a Saint, he doesn't *use* the Saint for his ends. It is the will of God or the Saint that controls the outcome—answers the pleadings. For the Christian it is also unthinkable that a good saint can also be used for doing evil. The Christian lives in discrete and absolute categories.

While Christians believe in possession, they almost always regard it as evil. As a rule they do not seek possession, except in rare and obscure sects. However, even in these sects it is God using them. It is never the practitioner using God. In the Christian snake-handling sects, the Holy Spirit possesses and protects the practitioner. Christians who claim to speak in tongues believe it is the Holy Spirit talking through them. While there are some similarities with Voodoo, the differences are glaringly obvious. The Voodooist both directs and is directed. The Christian is always directed.

The exchange between the Spirit and man in Voodoo is often an exchange of the material for the immaterial. Drums sound, dancing begins, blood and rum are given and the spirit enters the practitioner. The Voodooist first attracts the Spirit and then the Spirit possesses the practitioner. The Voodooist is aware that the spirit needs something from him and by giving the spirit what it wants he will receive what he wants. He feeds the spirit and the spirit feeds him. *The Voodooist realizes that the world between spirit and man is not opaque but translucent. For the Christian there is an almost impenetrable barrier between himself and his God.*

The "exchange" in Christianity is *passivity* for *assistance*. The "exchange" is made *by* the priest with minimal participation by the believer. More importantly, the blood sacrifice has already been made with the blood and body of Jesus. Thus, salvation (help) is vicarious. All has been worked out ahead of time—paid for by someone else. All the believer has to do is to have faith. This role is pathetic when compared to that of a Voodooist.

It is also sacrilegious for the believer to feel that he was controlling, feeding, or bribing God. And it would be sacrilege in many Christian sects to believe that God needed you, unless, of course, to perform his "Will." Of course, in Christianity and in Western civilization, claiming that you are an agent of God or a Saint is looked upon with suspicion or regarded as insane.

For the Christian, miracles are made by God. In fact, if God is not dead, He is at least impotent.

For the Voodooist "miracles" (magic) are made both by the spirit and the man. They are co-participants.

Christians are not allowed to practice magic, neither are they to divine. All is the will of God. God is active and man is passive. Man is made for the worship of God. In Voodoo, man is not simply made for the worship of God—he is also made for himself.

The dead, from the point of view of the Voodooist, are part of the living community. They are never really gone in the sense that we think. The dead are available to answer questions, provide guidance and take revenge.

The Voodooist has a very different notion of the extended family. The Voodooist's position is holistic and totalistic. It is a dialectic and not an irreconcilable dualism.

DIONYSUS—A BRIDGE BETWEEN TWO WORLDS?

Dionysus is not a simple invention of the Greeks. Most scholars agree that many of the rituals and concepts surrounding Dionysus-worship existed in the pre-Greek world, no doubt under different names. Some believe that Dionysus-worship simply incorporated early forms of Panism.

From the Greek historical point of view it is believed by some that Dionysus first appeared around the 8th century BC but didn't gain a powerful foothold until around the 7th century BC. Other scholars regard the Dionysus religion (cult) to be much older and that Dionysus was worshipped long before Apollo. In any event, we can be sure that the Dionysian religion was powerful and exerted great influence over intellectual and commoner alike both in ancient times as well as today.

From the Christian point of view Dionysus was the pinnacle of evil.[1] The nurses of Dionysus are wild women who play

---

[1]Nietzsche best sums up this distinction by his view on Christianity: "...Christianity was from the beginning, essentially and funda-mentally, life's nausea and disgust with life, merely concealed behind, masked by, dressed up as, faith in 'another' or 'better' life. Hatred of 'the world,' condemnations of the passions, fear of beauty and

significant roles in the rituals of this religion. Sex, including sodomy,[1] was practiced as was intoxication and animal sacrifice. These alone were sufficient for the new religion of Christianity to find fault. (Every new conquering group must both find fault as well as incorporate aspects of the older religion's deities. Of course, Christianity alone can't be blamed for this.)

Some aspects of the Dionysian religion—music, sex, drugs, alcohol, animal sacrifice, possession, dancing and frenzy—are closer to Voodoo than one might suspect at first glance. This would make sense as both religions are organic and lusty in nature and "ironically" both religions are evil according to the newcomer—Christianity.

Many anthropologists agree that all "primitive" religions have a similar base. This rests on the assumption that all peoples have similar needs and desires and that to a large extent these needs are primary and simplex.

---

sensuality, a beyond invented the better to slander this life, at bottom a craving for the nothing, for the end, for respite, for 'the Sabbath of Sabbaths'—all this always struck me, no less than the unconditional will of Christianity to recognize only moral values, as the most dangerous and uncanny form of all possible forms of a 'will to decline'..." From *The Birth of Tragedy*, translated by Walter Kaufman, *Basic Writings of Nietzsche*, Modern Library Edition, New York: 1968, p. 23. To call Christianity "progress" over the Roman and Greek religions raises the question of the quality of thinkers who have been influenced by Christianity.

[1]According to (Clement, 2, 29–30) Dionysos wanted to descend to Hades but did not know the way. A certain Prosymnos promised to show him in exchange for a sexual favor. Dionysos was receptive to the request, promised to yield to him if he would set him on his way, and confirmed his promise with an oath. After learning the way, Dionysos departed. On his return, he learned that Prosymnos had died. To discharge his obligation to his lover, Dionysos went to the tomb and committed a perversion. He cut off the branch of a fig tree, fashioned it into the shape of a male member and sat on the piece, thus carrying out his promise to the dead man. As a ritual reminder of this event, phalluses are set up to Dionysos throughout the world. From *The God of Ecstasy*, Arthur Evans, St. Martin's Press, New York: 1988.

The nature of these needs and their complexity is open to question. Simple fertility gods were not invented just to assure fertility, but served a greater purpose for mankind.

Anthropologists use a utility approach—that is, the gods were useful to man in a practical sense. This approach seems to please many people—particularly those who call themselves pragmatists and materialists. We believe that this definition includes dogmas and moralisms which are designed to provide solutions to the miseries of the world.

The demystification of the religious experience sank to its lowest level when the famed sociologist Durkheim posited that society had taken the place of God. If Durkheim's appraisal is correct, we can see, once more, that evolution—or "progress"—does not imply superiority.

We believe that all true religion serves the purpose of "getting high"—to use once common street slang. Being ecstatic—raising oneself up to God—was, at one time, at least as important as the assurance of fertility. Being full of God meant being full of life—and power.

POWER, FRENZY AND JOY

Women play significant roles both in Voodoo and Dionysian worship. They do not act solely as servants. They are also active and powerful participants, instigators and leaders. These roles are in direct contrast to the majority of Christian rituals and ceremonies. Christianity has historically regarded women as vile, evil and dirty.

Dionysus and his women are frenzied—possessed by forces. These forces are often thought of as joyful—full of the "joy of wine." Joy is also antithetical to the Christian world—the world of filth, sin, pain and suffering.

Frenzy, sometimes called madness, implies a loss of control—a danger for Christianity. The fear of frenzy or madness (devil possession) is so intense that many Christian writers feel that rock and roll is a sign that the Apocalypse of St. John is about to take place. Perhaps in a certain sense the Christians are correct—world views *do* change, but so what?

The practices of Dionysian worship—animal sacrifice, frenzy, possession, drugs, wine, sex, music and dancing—are remarkably similar to Raschke's list of Satanic attributes and acts.

Dionysus is not only a God of joy and creativity, he is also a God of destruction, death and change. As such the re-emergence of Voodooism and its practice by whites is a sign of a shift from the Christian view of the world to something quite different.

For those who see Christianity as superior to the Greek religions and to Voodooism, this view may seem regressive. We, however, believe the reverse—that Voodooism and the Dionysian Cult are superior to Christianity. Our view of time is not linear, but more spiral in nature.

This aside we must note that, if Voodooism and Dionysian practices are becoming more popular, they are becoming more popular with those who are also more scientific and high-tech than the originators.[1] This doesn't appear to be regressive; we will have to wait before we can be sure it is superior.

THE ATOMIZATION OF THE NUCLEAR FAMILY

The atomization of the nuclear family is a crucial issue for those concerned with Satanism. The shattering of systems of power and ownership is common during times of great change. Types of organizations come and go. To understand the fear of Raschke and his associates is simple. Christianity is all they know and they assume it and their brand of morality to be the basis of all progress. It seems that the worship of the State, the church and the nuclear family represents the Christian trinity which has done more to foster mediocrity than anything else in recent history. Of course, conformity and mediocrity is exactly what is desired.

Voodooism and the Dionysian cult foster a different notion of family. Incest is not uncommon, and the notion of family itself is very loose. What Raschke sees as the atomization of the nuclear family is really the development of a changing and shifting extended family that is so broad as to include dead ancestors. The global village is taking the place of the tract home and, as

---

[1]See, for example, *Count Zero* by William Gibson, Ace Books, New York: 1987, as an interesting example of this.

the culture prepares for the Apocalypse of St. John, we should expect more hysteria concerning the end of this era.

The nuclear family, often denoted by the phrase "traditional family values," allows well-defined lines of control (ownership). The nuclear family allows for much easier statistical manipulation than the extended family. The entire tax system of the United States is set up to accommodate this structure of ownership.

Identifiable characteristics have always been of interest for the State. However, ownership of slaves by the nobility—not the family or the division of labor—was the important issue. Slaves, of course, have always attempted to imitate the nobles—for example, look at the attempts of the middle-class in America. In this sense nuclear families make taxation, support and inheritance processes easier. The nuclear family intensified with the Industrial Revolution when pieces of the extended farm family broke off and moved to the city to work in the factories.

The nobles were concerned with property for the purpose of having an army as well as labor, assets, value and entertainment. Ownership gave the nobles the opportunity to be cruel, which some thinkers, like Nietzsche[1], believe is fundamental to the development of morality.

Voodoo from the white man's point of view simply means spirit, god or demon. The mystical world view of the Voodoo practitioner is wholistic. There is no separation between the material and spiritual world. While the Voodoo religion has "priests"—often called *Houngans* or *Bocor* depending on the type of magic (White or Black) performed—philosophically the Voodooist believes that direct contact with demons or spirits can be obtained without the direct help of the priest or of institutions. In these ways Voodoo is more democratic and less materialistic than Christianity. The Voodooist doesn't believe in original sin nor does he believe he was created for the sole purpose of worshipping God.

---

[1]*On the Genealogy of Morals.* Friedrich Nietzsche, translated by Walter Kaufman, *In the Basic Writings of Nietzsche*, Modern Library Edition, New York: 1968.

The Voodooist is fundamentally a pragmatist and an Ecstatic. He performs his rituals and prayers to get what he wants from this life—now. As such he is closer to what "white magicians" would call "black magic." "White magicians" claim that magic must only be performed for spiritual and altruistic reasons. If you perform magic for personal gain or for doing harm, you are practicing "black magic." This assertion is a result of Christian moral philosophy and has nothing to do with magic qua magic.

The Christian moral philosophy rests on self-abnegation and denial while Voodoo rests on self-fulfillment.

Voodoo is an animated world—not like ours which has separated God so far from His creation that neither seems vital. For the Voodooist and the Dionysian, God is immediate—here and now. Blood, the dance, the music and the world of the dead attest to God's immediacy.

While Voodoo is practical—it seeks results—Voodoo is also ecstatic. The Voodoo practitioner uses alcohol, music, animal sacrifice, dance and sometimes sex to create a frenzy so a spirit may enter the body. The spirit takes over the body and the person is no longer himself. To a Christian this is possession—an evil. The spirit can be that of a dead person or a deity and like some Dionysian rituals can also been seen as a salute to the dead.

Dead spirits are fed, and looked upon with awe and admiration. They are sought as guides as well as for revenge.

The Voodooist and the Dionysian are both acutely aware that life and death are intertwined. Not only is the relationship dialectic, it is also synthetic. Every birth is both a new beginning and a new end. As one merges more into life and meets death, something called madness or possession takes place. At that moment something new is created. The Dionysian cult was quite aware of the powers of the dead and the reality of the under-world. They were aware, like the Voodooist is aware, that life was affirmed by this strange and sometimes horrifying connec-tion with death that man could provoke through his rituals. The other world is necessary for the Voodooist—as it is for the Dionysian—so this world can exist at all. It is not simply fear which motivates the contact between the living and the dead, but the ever present fact of death within life. Life is not separated from death as it is for us moderns. These so-called primitive religions have a sense of the ecstatic qualities of reality as well as its continuity.

Where is the ecstatic in the modern world? Monday night football? Church on Sunday? A Saturday picnic? A pick-up bar? Our modern world, compared to the world of the Voodooist and the Dionysian, is quite uneventful. Even our religions demand that we be passive participants in the meager rituals we do have. Our entire Society is safety-passive oriented. Individual sports which are dangerous and require risk are heavily regulated and taxed. They are seen as pastimes for the rich, or as signs of rebellion.

From a strictly psycho-physiological point of view the worship of Dionysus and the practice of Voodoo demand a complete emotional release from the mundane qualities of day-to-day life.

Voodooism and Dionysus-worship require active participation where Christianity demands passivity. In this context the switch between the sacred and profane are reversed. In this context what we call active and madness are the sacred; what we call normal, passive, helpless, and dependent are the profane. What does the Christian see as sacred? What does he see as profane? The Christian sees the orgasmic release achieved in Voodooism and Dionysus-worship as cruel, evil, inhuman and mad. Our modern day psychologist would no doubt agree, although he would hold that insanity[1] was at the base of the behavior he observed. Thus, as we have mentioned previously demon possession is seen as a psychopathology.

As an experiment juxtapose the meek and the mild from the mad and the frenzied. Begin to juxtapose the sexual from the sexless. Begin to juxtapose the feeling of power from resignation. As you do this you will see the anemic condition of modern man as reflected by his life style and religion. Everything is either immoral, illegal or dangerous.

---

[1]Much of our definition of insanity is derived from religious beliefs. For example, demonic possession and insanity have similar qualities. If our religion were Voodoo, we might believe a person to be insane if he *didn't* become possessed by a demon.

Change—viewed as frenzy and madness—have always been seen by the homesteader as a threat to his sense of ownership and safety. He has neither the will nor the resources to protect himself. *Christianity is the religion of the nursing home.*[1]

Voodoo and the Dionysus cult attempt to imitate the power and glory of God. The living ritual is packed with grandeur, filled not simply with symbol, but with reality. To create and destroy, to dwell in life and death—this was religion. The world was alive with meaning—because the meaning was there—God dwelt, lived, and acted there—now, not simply in history or in dogma but as living reality.

---

[1]Goethe expresses this sentiments much better. In a letter to Frau von Stein, dated June 8, 1787 he says, "Also, I must say myself, I think it true that humanity will triumph eventually, only I fear that at the same time the world will became a large hospital and each will become the other's humane nurse."

CHAPTER NINE

SPIRITS, MAGICAL THEORY & PSYCHIC REPRESSION

There are three components to the corpus of magic the world over: the interaction of mind and mind, the interaction of mind and matter, and the communication with discarnate organisms, i.e., "spirits." Everything else, from speculation about astral planes to the proper arousal of kundalini, are details that sprout from these three subjects.

We were going to begin this chapter with a logical debate on the existence (or not) of spirits. Because, however, our earlier book (*Pacts with the Devil*, Falcon Press, Tempe, AZ: 1993) brought us some weird attacks from unexpected sources, we thought it *a propos* to discuss the American-European fear of the supernatural.

We are not just referring to the fear lodged at the heart of middle-class Judeo-Christian America, but in esoteric/occult groups themselves. We have a few "warnings" for prospective members of such groups based on our extensive experience.

We have both given examples earlier in the book on the schizoid response of individuals to spiritist phenomena. On the one hand, both mainstream religions and esoteric traditions (with a few exceptions) concern themselves with "life after death" in one form or another. This can be the celestial housing tracts of the Protestants or some form of reincarnation common to occult belief. *Either one presupposes the existence of spirits—there is simply no way around this.* And yet, many occult organizations

113

in the U.S.—the kind that attract middle-class white types—preach the idea of an afterlife, while at the same time dogmatically asserting that the "initiated" person *knows* that "spirits" are *really* "Jungian" archetypes or some sort of secondary personality split. This obvious contradiction seems to pass right over the heads of most of them, whether they are Wiccans, ceremonial magicians, or followers of Aleister Crowley. These are all groups who claim to practice "magic" including the evocation of invisible intelligences. After decades of experience with these groups we can state that, for the most part, *they do absolutely nothing of the sort.*

Jason tells the story of once having a conversation with a member of a "magical" group about poltergeists. This person asserted the hypothesis that all poltergeist phenomena were caused by the "unconscious" (whatever he meant by that) of disturbed adolescents living in the house. It was pointed out to him that a significant percentage of recorded and investigated cases occurred in places where there were either no children, as in the example told earlier in this book, or were in places where no one lived at all and the action was recorded on automatic cameras. The man's response was to stalk out of the room in a rage.

Why? What on earth is the cause of the emotional impact that this subject has on so many people—not just the average ignorant person on the street but individuals who claim to be seriously interested in "adeptship"? For anyone raised in a culture that suppresses psychic phenomena, and reduces serious discussion of non-human intelligences to "bible stories" (as Christian, Jewish, and Islamic cultures do), coming face to face with actual phenomena can be a catastrophic shock. The way such things are dealt with in most esoteric groups is no different, for the most part, than in a church. For such people, a single encounter with a "ghost", or with a UFO, can be the most devastating experience of a lifetime, *because it changes everything.*

More than once, on reviewing material written by qualified psychical researchers (psychologists, psychiatrists, physicists) we have run across remarks to the effect that they avoid investigating the claims of practitioners of the occult because "it's all compensation behavior to cover feelings of inferiority." Unfortunately this is true for ninety-five percent of the people involved in "magical" organizations. This is not to say that there aren't people who are intelligent and who seriously practice; there are, we have met them. Some are wealthy, some are public figures. If they happen to become associated with magical groups, they soon find there is nothing for them and they leave.

In a nutshell, someone who convinces themselves that magic is psychology and doesn't really work anyway can look in the mirror in the morning and see an adept. When confronted with people who have done the work and experienced "supernatural" results that have physically enhanced their lives, they can look in the same mirror and see a failure. It is easier to react with hostility than to change your way of living.

For example, we have had many experiences with the Wicca community in southern California. These groups were invariably dominated by extremely obese, loud women—Israel Regardie used to call them "tent women"—whose goal at any gathering seemed to be to push people around. This was usually accompanied by the sort of verbal moralizing ("that's *black magic*" or "he's incurring *bad karma*") that many of us can remember from Sunday school. These people claim to be nature mystics, but the clinical obesity, poor hygiene, chain smoking and chronic bickering tell a very different story. Jason was once shown a particularly pompous and moralizing article in a "Neo-Pagan" magazine, and in annoyance he asked (about the author), "Does she weigh four hundred pounds?" His friend replied in some indignation that he knew her and she was quite thin. Looking him in the eye Jason asked, "What's wrong with her?" After a moment's silence: "Well, she's kind of cross-eyed and has a neurological disorder."

It is not our intention to be cruel here, merely to point out some unpleasant truths about the "New Age" or any other movement. If you join a magical order—or a church—and at the first meeting find yourself in a room full of people with only one eye, you'd better consider the possibility that you have really joined a support group for one-eyed people. We have picked on Wicca here, but we could have used almost any group—from Theosophists to the various followers of Crowley or the Golden

Dawn(s) or LaVey—with only slightly different "common elements" for each group.

The point being, that the stated goal or agenda of many of these groups is in no way the real one. On the one hand you have clinically obese chain-smokers claiming to be "one with nature"; on another you have Crowleyites, whose motto is "Do What Thou Wilt" but worry themselves sick about whether old Aleister approved of abortion or even birth control. The circle of psychic athletes that Crowley once envisioned is now dominated by religious cranks who have found the messiah "and behold! he is a dead Englishman who shaveth his head!" In groups of people whose main goal is to stop feeling inferior the *real* pursuit of higher spiritual abilities is not encouraged. It requires a lot of work—something else to be avoided—and if someone does achieve something in this line "good reasons" are always found to ease them out of the group.

Obviously, such people, even if truly interested, cannot handle the emotional stress and sometimes quite justified fear produced by spirit phenomena. The possible benefits are irrelevant as many of the people described above have long resigned themselves to lives of borderline poverty and working in the company mail room.

Another reason for hostility—or at least indifference—toward spirit phenomena is that most of the members of these groups want nothing more than to dress up on a Saturday night, do a little religious ritual and then have a few beers. Nothing wrong with this if serious work is also included in the curriculum, but it almost never is. In fact, psychic or supernatural experience is the last thing they really want. Add to this an absolutely cavernous ignorance of the literature of psychic phenomena—which one would think would be of primary interest—and you have an "occult movement" with all the substance of a hot-air balloon.

Contrast this with the Voodoo subculture's attitude. Like all real magic it developed to meet genuine physical and emotional needs. Whether a person practices alone or is the client of a *Santero*, *Palero* or *Bocor*, solid results are expected and often urgently needed. We have related some of our own experiences regarding these—"help" was given even during the research for this book. On several occasions, Jason was at a loss as to where to locate the local botanicas that he knew existed. During *each* of these times, in restaurants or social gatherings he encountered a stranger who would without being asked, and in the middle of a totally unrelated conversation, mention that he had seen a botanica at such-and-such a location. Jason would note it down, and work on the book could proceed.

We will begin serious discussion of spirits with a quote from Carl Jung that we have also used in *Pacts with the Devil:*

> I once discussed the proof of identity for a long time with a friend of William James, Professor Hyslop, in New York. He admitted that, all things considered, all these metapsychic phenomena could be explained better by the hypothesis of spirits than by the qualities and peculiarities of the unconscious. And here, on the basis of my own experience, I am bound to concede he is right. In each individual case, I must of necessity be skeptical, but in the long run I have to admit that the spirit hypothesis yields better results in practice than any other.

We believe that it becomes clear to anyone who reads material by and about Jung—especially material not published until after his death, that he believed not only in the literal existence of spirits, but in a substantial chunk of what is traditionally considered occult. In other words, while *you* may believe that Jungian archetypes are "all in your head" *he* most emphatically did not.

For an overview of the history of investigation into spirit phenomena by trained scientific researchers as well as a wealth of anecdotal material we recommend a number of the works of British author Colin Wilson, especially *Poltergeist* and *Beyond the Occult.* These are particularly useful because of their encyclopedic nature and because of Mr. Wilson's narrative of how he came to the conclusion that spirits were not always mental phenomena, but actually existed.

This is not to say that the distinction is always simple, it is not. If a spirit appears to you in a dream, is it "real" or is it you? For the vast majority of people the answer is determined strictly by cultural programming. For example, our concepts of individuality *seem* natural, but in fact depend entirely on where and how we are raised. For example, consider the view that the Communist Chinese are "robotic." We are just as robotic as they are—just as much and just as little. We feel the center of consciousness inside our skulls. We consider this to be a fact. We can *physically feel* it. And yet other cultures historically have *physically felt* consciousness to be in such places as the heart, solar plexus and even the liver. There is now some controversy over whether the brain is actually the location of the "mind" or whether this elusive thing has no single location in the body.

So, let us explore the complications of a mind and a personality without a body (as we understand it), that is, a spirit. Almost every culture enumerates different types and levels of spirits—a kind of non-physical ecology—with predators, scavengers, parasites and other functionaries. This has often been ridiculed as unsophisticated pantheism, but an overview of the case histories of hauntings, possessions and weird spontaneous encounters implies that the old models may be the most accurate we so far have.

When we say that both our experience and the evidence of history supports the spirit hypothesis is definitely not to say that we literally "believe" in the structure of either the Afro-Caribbean pantheon or the European demonologies. Far from it. We have read books by several "anglos" who have adopted the "pure" *Ifa* religion of the *Yorubas* lock, stock and barrel, with moralisms and formalized mythology intact and found them annoying. The great virtue of Voodoo in contrast to other paths is direct experience and the pursuit of results.

What we do suspect, is that "magic names" work like any others: If you keep calling, say, *Baron Samedi* in a graveyard to kill an enemy, something eventually may come along that can kill your enemy and will consent to answer to that name, not just for you, but eventually for others as well. Whether this "something" is already there, or *forms* as the Tibetans sometimes assert, is anyone's guess.

Jason implied earlier that he feels that his involvement with Voodoo came about because he was in the neighborhood *where the spirits lived.* As someone born with "mediumistic" abilities, he acted as a kind of beacon and "they" came to visit *him.* In other words, a spontaneous encounter with entities that responded to Afro-Caribbean names is unlikely to have occurred in Idaho or Taiwan, but might have more easily in Florida.

What is dealt with in Voodoo, and indeed in classical Paganism of the Greek or Roman variety are not single "Gods", but families of spirits of a related nature. One estimate of the number of different Guedes (a death *Loa* like Baron Samedi) that could be listed in Haiti was in the thousands. There are a number of different Erzulies also, both good and "bad" and the number of Eshus or Elegguas is astronomical if you combine Cuban and Brazilian material. If you start examining the notion of spirits seriously, as opposed to some kind of mythological symbol, you are dealing with a proliferation, a multitude of beings of varying degrees of intelligence, power, and usefulness ranging from an organism no smarter than a mouse to the daemons and gods of religious thought.

In Voodoo (indeed in all *traditional* magic) spirits are dealt with as you would any friend or business associate of flesh and blood. They are spoken to clearly, greeted in a way that betokens respect, and paid for the requested service. This is an important point that cannot be glossed over. Once you discover that the phenomena is real and not a "psychodrama" (as Anton LaVey liked to call it) you must ask yourself what sort of thing such an organism would want. Tradition also answers this. Generally speaking it is some kind of organic food, just like any other animal. The phobias in our voracious meat-eating modern culture against blood sacrifice, most commonly of *chickens* for heaven's sake, is inconsistent, irrational, and goes right back to the aforementioned fear of the supernatural.

The Los Angeles writer, Michael Ventura, in his excellent Introduction to *Santeria, A Practical Guide to Afro-Caribbean Magic* by Luis Manuel Nunez (Spring Publications, 1992) points out that the horror of doing a ritual for oneself, not just the possible result of such an act, contributes to the fear reaction. He goes on to say that our Judeo-Christian culture has had its relationship to the supernatural taken over for it by rabbis, priests and ministers and aside from simple prayer (begging) most people feel that to perform the full invocation of a "god" for oneself is *in and of itself* a sinister act.

This caught us off guard when we read it, because of our own decades-long hands-on involvement with ritual. And yet, Jason can remember the horrified reaction of a man toward the book, *Aleister Crowley's Illustrated Goetia* (Falcon Press, Tempe, AZ: 1992). One of the authors (Lon Milo DuQuette) had described how he drew a magic circle on the ground and proceeded to attempt to call up a spirit. It was not the alleged results that so disturbed the reader, but the act of engaging in the ritual itself. Some sort of a Baptist, he had never done anything but sing hymns and be talked at by preachers in his life, thus to even attempt such a thing on one's own behalf was perversion. He kept shaking his head saying "I'd never do that, I'd never do that."

And how much more disturbing the blood sacrifice added on top of this. By no means do all of the rituals or spells require such an thing, and when they do, the blood is given to the "god" and the animal is usually cooked and eaten by the participants. In addition, such things as fruit, vegetables and grains are also common offerings, indeed, entire prepared meals. (The reader should realize that the ancient Jews had no problems with offerings. In fact to the horror of some modern Orthodox Jews is the fact that animal sacrifice would begin immediately with the establishment of the Third Temple. It is fascinating to realize that many of the 613 commandments have to do with offerings, sex, marriage, slavery and violence. Few modern Jews would feel comfortable associating with their religion in its authentic form.)

Raw meat from a butcher shop can do as a substitute, but there are only a few circumstances where it is the offering of choice.

We remind the reader of the description of the poltergeist haunting earlier in the book. This, as all the ancient writers on the subject agree, implies the existence of a body *of some kind*, since kinetic energy is produced and physical matter is manipulated. Something similar can be said for the far smaller energy required to influence another mind or make someone sick. How much kinetic energy is required to create a blood clot, or transfer a virus?

In light of the above, we would like to emphasize that when we speak of an offering of whatever nature, in the practice of magic, it is *not* symbolic. Magic is a technology of interacting with, and influencing the phenomenal world on a desired level, physical or otherwise. Spirits are organisms, too, and even if they don't appear to *eat* something, they certainly *want* something. This can sometimes be a certain action in which they vicariously participate for their own enjoyment, like an act of sex, or cigar-smoking. The magician receives gifts likewise. He partakes of the spirit's ability to transcend time and space through clairvoyance and divination. Profound emotional changes and changes in "luck" and even intelligence and talent have been achieved through evocation techniques.

We give them the benefit of the physical and they give us the benefit of the ethereal. A fair exchange, not the slavish relationship so feared by the Judeo-Christian-Islamic establishment.

We have said that magic is technology, and this is so, but not the sort that our Victorian materialist culture understands, nor that of Quantum physics. It involves a relationship between mind and matter that we do not accept, except in the fantasy world of "faith." While it is technology, it is also art, just as sculpture and architecture are both art and technology. As an art, it requires inborn talent, specifically some sort of psychic ability or mediumship. With this in mind the following chapter is particularly important, and serious effort should be made to master the techniques described, especially the induction of trance states.

CHAPTER TEN

DIVINATION TECHNIQUES

While divination is integral to all forms of magical practice, in the various Voodoo traditions it is more important than most, since any divination is an invocation of the gods.

In their original form many of the traditional African methods of divination are complex beyond belief. This is complicated by the fact that even in their new world forms much is still passed on verbally and therefore genuinely secret and not just obscure.

As this book is aimed at the self-taught practitioner who is not raised in a *Santeria* or *Macumba* community, we are limiting the methods to those that are both effective and relatively simple.

There are five basic methods of divination used in the Afro-Caribbean traditions:

1. **TAROT CARDS.** These are used primarily by the magicians of Haiti, although cards are used in *Macumba* and *Santeria* as well. There is also a pack called "the Spanish playing cards" which evolved from the Tarot, but have the trumps and queens removed, leaving only forty-eight cards. We will not explain the Tarot here, as that would take an entire book. Those of you interested may purchase a standard deck (the Rider/Waite deck is most popular among beginners) and many books of instruction are available. For those interested in advanced instruction on serious divination with the cards and their magical connections refer to *Sex Magic, Tantra & Tarot: The Way of the Secret Lover* by Christopher S. Hyatt, Ph.D. and Lon Milo DuQuette (Falcon Press, 1991).

2. **THE PENDULUM.** This tool is not normally associated with Voodoo. In fact the pendulum was and is used for spirit communication in Africa, and because of its versatility and simplicity, and because it can be used with any other style of divination, we include it here.

3. **THE OBI**. These consist of four pieces of cola nut. Replacements for this hard-to-find item will be suggested although those who live in New York or Miami may be able to get the authentic item. One of the most basic and simple methods of speaking with the spirits.

4. **THE CARACOLES (COWRY SHELLS).** This is the most complex and ancient of the divination systems and is presented in a greatly simplified form created especially for this book.

5. **POSSESSION (ALTERED STATES OF CONSCIOUS-NESS).** This is the most difficult thing for people in our culture to deal with. Here we will concentrate on auto-hypnotic techniques, principally because spirit possession tends to occur—and is only desirable—in group situations. Possession phenomena will be mentioned, however, along with advice on how to use it—and get rid of it.

THE USE OF THE PENDULUM

The pendulum is a balanced weight suspended from a piece of string or a fine chain. A homemade pendulum can be made with rings or steel nuts. Particular care should be taken so that it is as balanced as possible. The authors use professionally made dowser's pendulums, usually made from machined brass or copper. They are either bullet or onion shaped, some with hollow spaces inside for what, in dowsing, is called "the witness." This is identical in concept to the magical link.

We have seen pendulums for sale in occult shops aimed at the "new age" audience that were made from quartz crystal points attached to a chain. In our opinion these are nearly useless as they are off balance and too light. We recommend that you take the trouble to find one that is professionally made. They are inexpensive, usually costing U.S.$20.00 or less.

The use of the pendulum is quite simple in theory, but you may find it takes some time and patience to "get it to work" for you. The temptation to "make" the pendulum tell you what you want to hear must be resisted.

For the purposes of spirit communication we have found the best method to be to have your arm (whichever you normally use to write with) solidly anchored, elbow on a table, or, if you are sitting on the floor in a cross-legged position, on your knee.

The classic method used to "train" the pendulum—or rather to train your mind in the use of the pendulum—is to give it a little swing forward and back away from you in a straight line. You then ask the pendulum to give you a motion that indicated "yes" or "positive." The response is generally a clockwise circle, but this may vary. The process is repeated for "no" or negative. In the event that this fails to work, an alternative is to *tell* the pendulum that a clockwise circle is "yes" and deliberately swing the tool in that direction, repeating the process with "no."

Most people who try this will get a response that becomes more sure and dependable with practice. A few will be instantly proficient. Others will feel unable to use the pendulum at all. If this happens, put the pendulum away until you feel some later "urge" to pick it up again. We have found that once the suggestion is planted, some people who demonstrated no ability, will, after some time suddenly find themselves proficient—with no intervening practice.

The test of any divinatory system is the accuracy of the information it provides. Until you have confidence in this or any other method the answers should always be tested and not just assumed to be correct.

Another classic method of using the pendulum is with a kind of ouija board set up, with the letters of the alphabet and numbers written in either an arc or a circle with lines drawn from these to the center of the board. The pendulum is held over this and questions are asked to which words are spelled out in response. This can be quite time-consuming and a strain on the arm. Occasionally boards like this can be found in stores ready made. Also books on radiesthesia (the name for pendulum dowsing) sometimes contain charts of this kind that can be copied for use with a pendulum.

THE OBI

The *Obi* consist of four flat objects that can be easily tossed. There must be a difference between each side—generally one is darker than the other. Traditionally the *Obi* have been four lobes of the cola nut, or four pieces of fresh coconut. A good substitute are the flat glass beads used for floral arrangements; these can be found in large import stores. White circles of paper can be glued to one side to form the color differentiation (paint tends to flake off glass). Alternatively, coins can be used.

A question is asked that can be answered in some positive-negative fashion. This is actually more complex than "yes," or "no," and, if the *Obi* are thrown several times in succession a rather complex prediction can be achieved.

There are five possible patterns in which the *obi* can fall in a single throw, each with a title and a meaning:

Generally the *Obi* are thrown once for any specific question, although a series of questions may be posed.

There are two exceptions to this: If *Alafia* (peace) or *Etawa* (struggle) comes up you must throw a second time to complete the answer. This only applies on a first throw. There are no more than two tosses. You may for example throw *Etawa* and for the second throw get *Alafia*. That (struggle becoming peace) is the answer. There are no further throws for that particular question.

The basic process is quite simple: Place yourself in a meditative and serious frame of mind, and cleanse the room in which you are working. In some Brazilian methods a fine chain or cord is placed in a circle around the area in which the *Obi* are to be thrown to define the sacred space. In *Santeria* the *Obi* are often cleansed in a bowl of exorcised water to make them pure. After asking the spirits, or a particular spirit to attend to your question, the *Obi* are tossed and the answer noted. The *Obi* can also be used in conjunction with the pendulum to gain more detail on the nature of the answer.

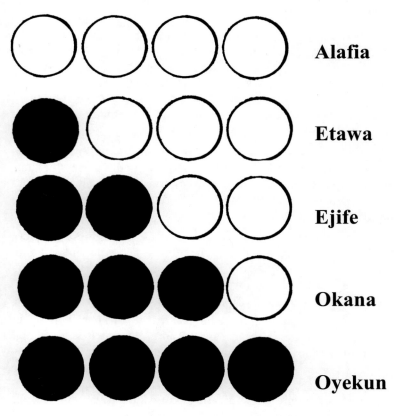

THE OBI AND THEIR NAMES

THE MEANINGS OF THE ODU

The five patterns in which the *Obi* can land are called the *Odu*. The divinatory meanings of the *Odu* are:

ALAFIA (Peace). Broadly speaking, this is serenity and balance. The reader not familiar with the *Obi* will assume that this is the most auspicious *Odu* in the group because it consists of the most "positive" energy. In fact this is not quite the case since it is considered rather unbalanced. It is quiet and serene, yes, but if there is too much of it, it is also lassitudinous and unfocused. Altogether a quiet, good omen, especially when it appears after a period of struggle. If *Alafia* appears on a first throw, the answer is incomplete and the *Obi* must be tossed again to complete the answer.

ETAWA (Struggle). As the name suggests, *Etawa* represents conflict. It could be conflict directly with a person or persons or struggle with a difficult situation. Confusion, things not in their proper place. This is a major or minor event depending on the subject of the question. Like *Alafia*, it is incomplete if it turns up on the first throw, and a second toss must be made to complete the answer, for conflict always has an outcome.

EJIFE (Balance). This, of all the *Odu*, is the one that is considered the most auspicious. It represents the perfect balance of dark and light forces to create a harmonious, perfectly functioning situation. Please note the difference between this attitude and the Christian or Islamic one.

OKANA (Some good, some bad). This *Odu* one might consider the omen of the average day. It means that generally speaking all is (more or less) well. It implies that one element or incident may cause a less than satisfactory flow of events.

OYEKUN (Darkness). In the translation from the *Yoruba* this means "Full Twilight" but we have called it Darkness here as, to our minds, it reflects the meaning more clearly. It is the polar compliment to *Alafia*, being the negative power at its very height. In *Santeria* tradition, this *Odu* implies influences of the very worst kind. It is said that the divination should be abandoned at once, and a candle lit asking the protection of your ancestors. In its most benign sense, it can mean that the question cannot be answered

THE MEANINGS OF THE OMO ODU

If either *Alafia* (peace) or *Etawa* (struggle) are thrown first, a second throw must be made to complete the answer. Each of these combinations have separate meanings. These are called *Omo Odu,* meaning "children of the Odu."

We will begin with the *Omo Odu* resulting from a first throw of *Alafia*:

ALAFIA + ALAFIA. This is the overwhelming presence of the "light" element, and the danger is laziness or drunkenness, or, on a milder note, complacency. If some task is to be accomplished, sobriety (in every sense) and concentration are urged.

ALAFIA + ETAWA. This indicates a time of peace, contemplation, rest and planning before a test or struggle. It advises clear-headedness and emotional coolness if victory is desired in the coming difficult situation.

ALAFIA + EJIFE. This is a good omen that combines cool-headedness and balance. It implies a "what will be, will be" attitude, and "what will be" is probably good.

ALAFIA + OKANA. This implies that no matter how much serenity and planning are represented by *Alafia*, *Okana* will throw a wrench into the works with one tiny unforeseen factor. Largely negative, implying great caution, or abandonment of the activity in question to another time.

ALAFIA + OYEKUN. The sudden unexpected occurrence of disaster, like going to the mailbox and being shot by a sniper. A warning of extreme caution, and also a warning that the dark elements cannot be calculated or accounted for.

Here are the *Omo Odu* resulting from a first throw of *Etawa*:

ETAWA + ALAFIA. This implies a peaceful, satisfying situation that can only come about after hard work and perhaps competition and struggle. You must earn your reward.

ETAWA + ETAWA. As the name of the *Odu* implies this is struggle after struggle. This is a situation of unrelenting effort before the desired goal is achieved. Any slacking means probable failure. In a lesser sense it can mean that nothing goes right no matter what you do.

ETAWA + EJIFE. This represents struggle or effort leading to perfect balance and a successful outcome.

ETAWA + OKANA. No matter how hard we work, our plans are fouled by one little event or element. This can mean frustration and failure after hard work, or in a more minor mode, working for perfection and getting mediocrity.

ETAWA + OYEKUN. The presence of *Oyekun* makes this black as the ace of spades. We struggle and struggle only to meet inevitable defeat. Our own energy is even used against us to our undoing. Find an honorable way to retreat—or just duck.

THE TABLE OF IFA: THE CARACOLES

The use of cowry shells is the central technique of divination in *Santeria* and *Macumba*. The Haitian variety has a different national origin, and as a result of its history was isolated for nearly a century (they were denied diplomatic status by both the U.S. and Europe for a century because of white outrage at the idea of a successful slave revolt). The magic from Cuba, Puerto Rico, and the Virgin Islands spread to America (*Santeria*), and this, like the tradition in Brazil (*Macumba*) had its roots in the *Yoruba* culture.

In the simplest version of its original form sixteen cowry shells were used as sacred divinatory tools. Several other objects were pulled blindly out of a bag to help determine the positive or negative slant on the reading.

All of this was usually done on a beautifully carved wooden tray with the face of *Ifa* himself staring out from the top (in Africa) or on a consecrated straw mat (in the U.S.). In Brazil a circle of chain or cord is used to define the sacred space.

One of the lords of the crossroads is called upon (see the chapter on Legba/Eshu) and the shells are thrown one or more times. The shells have been cut and filed so that they fall flat on one side or another like flipping a coin. There is another method using sixteen flat pieces of metal attached to a chain which is tossed rather like a horseshoe. To our knowledge this particular method is now used only in Africa, but it may still be practiced in some parts of Brazil.

In the case of the cowry shells the serrated openings on the bottom were considered the mouths of the spirits, and only the shells facing up were counted to determine the answer.

Each number—from one to sixteen—of possible upward facing "mouths" had a "proverb" and a mythological story attached to it. There were also cleansing spells called *Ebbos* attached to each number. In addition, according to some authorities, there are as many as *five hundred* "secret" meanings attached to the system that to this day is passed on only orally.

For this reason we have create this simplified method that does not compromise the spirit of the system and is still possible for the beginner to learn. We emphasize that what we present here is a new adaptation of the "Table of Ifa" and not what one would be taught by an initiated *Santero* or *Macumba* priest.

HOW TO CONSTRUCT THE ORACLE

You will need sixteen cowry shells. (The traditional number is eighteen, but two are not used, being considered guardians of the oracle.) For the non-initiate practitioner, sixteen is all you need. These may be obtained from hobby shops and import stores, although I am told that their availability tends to be seasonal. The shells should be small, not the large kind often seen in coastal souvenir shops, about the size of a dime or nickel. The humped backs of the shells must be ground down flat so that the shells have an even chance of landing on either side.

If you live in an area with African import stores, or real Botanicas, you may be able to find these shells easily, possibly with the hump already worn down, thus saving a great amount of painstaking work.

You will also need a circular or square tray with a lip around the edge to prevent the shells from flying off when tossed. The tray must be square or circular and not oval or rectangular, as the flat area will be divided into four equal parts when the board is finished. The tray should be something more than a foot in diameter—eighteen inches to two feet is a good size. A medium sized pizza tray works well and can be purchased any place that sells kitchen utensils.

Paint the following design (or glue a copy of it) on the tray. (The colors, divisions and signs were determined through a seance using the pendulum, so this is a divination system produced through divination!)

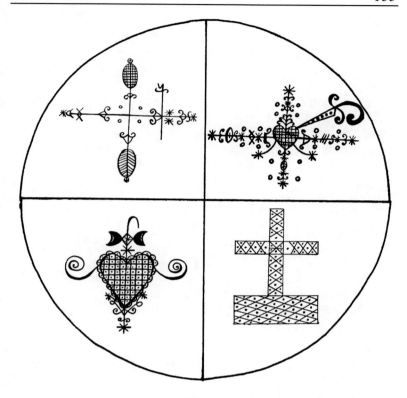

BOARD DESIGN FOR SHELL DIVINATION

In the upper left hand corner is the symbol of Legba, the lord of the crossroads, who opens doorways and conveys information. His symbol is painted white on a black background. This segment of the board represents positive, or benign male energy, and is particularly important in questions related to communication, travel, contracts and "white magic."

In the lower left hand corner is the symbol of Erzulie. It is painted black on an orange ground. This is positive female energy, and is important in questions regarding relationships, inspiration and all things related to the positive aspect of the astrological concept of Venus.

In the upper right hand corner is the symbol of Erzulie Dantor, also called Erzulie Ge-Rouge ("the red eyed"). This is painted black on a white ground. This quarter of the board is important to matters of anger, hatred, jealousy and feelings of oppression. It is negative female energy.

In the lower right hand corner is the symbol of Baron Samedi, which is painted black on red. This quarter represents negative or aggressive male energy. It is important in matters of "black magic," winning in competitions, defeating enemies, and all questions regarding death. Ironically Baron Samedi is also a healer, so this quarter of the board also speaks of regaining health from illness.

THE MEANINGS OF THE ODU

The meanings given here are based upon the sixteen "proverbs." These meanings are also called *Odu* in the *Yoruban* language. These descriptions were developed for the system in this book and are based on the traditional meanings.

Each divinatory meaning has a number from one to sixteen. This number represents the number of shells with their "mouths" upright.

1. Mediocrity. Nothing much is happening or developing in this situation. Neither harm nor good.

2. Probable disagreement, competition, or conflict, possibly with a close associate or loved one. Contention and strife. Patience and serenity advised.

3. A conflict or argument leading to a deeply regrettable outcome. Implies the possibility of violence, accident or suicide as a result. Any conflict is to be avoided if possible. A good time to pursue solitary activity.

4. A mystery to be dealt with. The question cannot properly be answered as it is "covered over" by circumstances. Also implies unconscious motives and the world of dreams that cannot be handled with logic. Cultivate intuition and consult the spirits.

5. Having to do with the force of life itself, blood, health, fitness. In another sense the most basic and primitive motivations of a person or situation. A chance to deal with the fundamental forces of your life, physical or spiritual.

6. Seeking or standing up for the truth. A situation where no amount of subterfuge by you or another can hide the truth of a statement or situation. Warns also to beware of lies by others.

7. The fundamental origin of any serious problem. It means you must deal with the hard to face basic facts of any recurring problem, either with yourself or others.

8. This says that the power of your thought is the most important factor in this matter. It can control and change circumstances and even your bodily health. The power of mind over matter.

9. What you love best is killing you. This could be a bad love affair, a drug addiction or anything similar. It advises that this love must be given up. In another direction it can also mean that a close friend is betraying you behind your back.

10. The origin of a curse. The source of bad luck or "karma" must be dealt with. Guilt from the past must be eliminated. The source of bad energy and events must be eliminated from your life. You may also have been literally cursed and have to deal with that on its own level.

11. You are attempting to do something with inadequate tools or preparation. Whether within yourself or in the physical world you must have the right tools for the right job. Prepare more conscientiously and you will succeed.

12. There is conflict, even amounting to all out war. No relaxation is possible in this situation if victory is to be achieved. This could be in the outside world or within yourself.

13. Physical and/or spiritual purification is called for. Meditation, diet and environment are to be cleansed for improvement.

14. You are in a group or family where people envy you. Watch your words and your back.

15. Enthusiasm, religious experience, an overwhelmingly impressive and possibly joyous event. Whether positive or negative, the experience or emotion is potentially life changing.

16. Your intelligence and effectiveness will be multiplied if you seek other advice or sources of information. The answers are there, but you do not have all the information yet. Spread out your lines to bring in information. Network. Listen.

HOW TO USE THE ORACLE

Wash your hands thoroughly before handling the shells, mentally imagining that this also cleanses your spirit.

Place the tray on an altar or on the floor. Greet the Master of the Crossroads and ask him to open a dialogue with the spirits so that they may answer you clearly and truthfully (see the section on Legba/Eshu).

If the divination is for another person present, they should be allowed to hold the shells and think about their question. The shells are then handed back to the diviner, held in both hands in a prayer-like position and tossed onto the tray.

First, count the number of shells that "speak." This is the overall general answer to the question. It may be a direct answer, or take the form of advice, rather like the *I Ching*.

Now, examine and note each quarter division of the tray. Count the shells that speak in each separate section. Again this is to be done for each section as a separate answer. Any "speaking" shells that straddle the dividing black lines that quarter the tray are to be counted for the overall answer, but ignored for the reading of the four quarters.

The quarter of the board with the most speaking shells indicates the dominant force in the question. while the quarter with the fewest shells indicates the weakest force. The quarter with the most positive *Odu,* may show the way out of any implied difficulty.

Thus the shells can be read like a simplified astrological chart. For complex questions, this process can be gone through two or more times, but beware of trying to get the answer you want to hear. Any warnings given by the spirits can be quite serious.

As an example, if you receive a good *Odu* for the overall answer, but the majority of the "speaking" shells are in the upper right quarter ruled by Erzulie Dantor, it implies success, but with a great deal of emotional turmoil and contention in the process. The specific *Odu* contained in that quarter also adds more detail about the nature or cause of the turmoil.

With practice, this can form a detailed story in much the same way as the tarot and with the ability to give advice that typifies *I Ching* readings.

POSSESSION & ALTERED STATES OF CONSCIOUSNESS

The subject of possession is associated with terror and the demonic in Christian culture. (This apparently excludes "letting Jesus into your heart" which sounds suspiciously like demonic possession to us.)

Possession in the Voodoo traditions almost always occurs in group rituals, frequently after hours of preliminary ceremonies. While the average westerner assumes that possession is hypnosis or fraud, there are many documented cases of hostile witnesses who were spontaneously possessed while observing these rituals in Haiti, Brazil and other places. Almost without exception they suffered the amnesia, increased strength, and sometimes invulnerability to fire that typify the qualities of the spirit that claimed them. They would speak in the language of the place—whether they knew it or not—and serve the celebrants with advice, healing, and so forth as though a native. This usually caused great embarrassment and anger to the Christian skeptics to whom this occurred.

It may surprise the reader that religious possession, long considered psychosis by condescending observers, or demonic possession by meddling missionaries, is now considered normal by many ethnologists and appears in every culture where it is not suppressed or punished—as it is in ours.

Dr. Wade Davis, author of *The Serpent and The Rainbow,* was honest enough to admit that he had witnessed phenomena involving possession that he could not explain, and courageous enough (considering his academic standing) to admit that the existence of spirits could not be disproved by science.

The film-maker Maya Deren, in *Divine Horsemen,* an account of her study of Haiti, also tells how she experienced spontaneous possession by the spirit Erzulie on several occasions, acting as the goddess for the celebrants. Her amnesia after the experience was absolute. Ms. Deren seemed to suffer some embarrassment in writing about this, as she hid this remarkable experience in the back of the book in an appendix.

The symptoms of possession are roughly these: A numbing of the limbs, sometimes accompanied by involuntary movements or even convulsions. If this occurs the person undergoing the experience should only be touched enough to prevent him from injuring himself. Sometimes the experience may end at this point and no full possession takes place, otherwise another personality will manifest and a name should be demanded by the person presiding over the ritual. If cooperation is received, then the spirit can be consulted while in the body of the possessed person. If the spirit is unruly, or disoriented, or hostile, it should be banished firmly and with authority by the presiding magician. Traditionally bells are used for this as well as sprinklings with some consecrated liquid. This is an ancient practice in many cultures and one of hundreds copied by the Christian church.

The formerly possessed person may feel physically exhausted afterwards, even for as much as a day. It is important that the spirit give verbal consent to leave the person, and not enter him again unless called by ritual.

For those who work alone, possession is highly unlikely and rather undesirable. However, if one is to attempt it, the western Judeo-Christian resistance to trance states in general—at least the kind involved in magic—must be overcome for the best results.

At its most successful, auto-hypnotic meditation techniques combined with magical ritual will enhance psychic functioning, and provide startling psycho-physical reactions that anthropologists refer to as "ecstatic." This is the sort of thing people of tradition experience when they travel to "the spirit world." Genuine out-of-body experiences occasionally but rarely occur.

To learn self-hypnosis requires patience and a commitment of time, but the technique itself is actually rather simple. It is possible to learn from a commercially produced tape, or by visiting a professional hypnotist. We recommend that tapes be used as little as possible and the practitioner use his or her own voice. A full somnambulistic state is not the goal here, nor would it be useful when working alone.

The elaborate preparations used by both authors in our joint work were described earlier. A much simpler technique used by S. Jason Black for solitary work will be outlined here.

Sit in a straight-backed chair (do *not* lie down)in front of a table about the height of a desk. This can be done sitting cross-legged on the floor, but only if you can do this for up to an hour without discomfort.

Before this exercise, perform a cleansing ritual. The table should be set up as a magical altar, and lit by candles even if in the daytime. The focus of the altar—whatever else may be on it—should be a crystalline object that reflects the light of the candles. Jason uses a polished quartz crystal ball on a brass stand. As these can be expensive, quartz crystal points a little larger than your thumb are also useful. If you have a ball of lead-crystal glass, use that. The important thing is that it refract the light and quartz does that much better than clear glass.

Face the crystal with your eyes fixed on it and tell yourself in a whisper that you cannot take your eyes from it. Tell yourself that with each breath you take and each word you speak you are going deeper and deeper into trance. Tell yourself that your body is becoming rigid and unable to move, but utterly without tension of any kind.

Sound can be used as a background if you wish. Recordings of Tibetan monastic chants, for example, are available and are quite useful in this regard.

You will find your breathing changing at various times during this process. You should attempt to control and slow it only in the beginning. The deeper you go into trance the more you will find that your breathing changes in unexpected ways without interfering with your state. Let this happen. It may become swift, or shallow, or slow almost to imperceptibility. Similar descriptions can be found in the writings of Tantrik Yoga.

While staring at the crystal, tell yourself that your mind is lifting from your body into a higher, causal plane of being. Then tell yourself that you will count from one to ten, and, when you reach ten, all of your spiritual and psychic centers will open. Make this count slowly, one number to each breath.

Let the trance deepen. Do nothing for a while, and place no time limits on yourself unless absolutely necessary. For Jason, this exercise averages forty-five minutes to an hour.

When you feel your trance has deepened, tell yourself again that you will count from one to ten. In addition, suggest that in the crystal is the gateway to the spirit world and the being that you seek to communicate with (if that is indeed your goal).

When you reach ten you will be even deeper in trance, and pass through the gateway to the spirit kingdom.

When this is done, relax into the hypnogogic experience of speaking with the spirit. Make no attempt to prejudge what you will see.

At any time during this process you may give yourself permission to move enough to use a pendulum, or read an appropriate invocation from a book. Do this slowly, so as not to spoil the state of trance. Return to the relaxed seated position when done.

When you consider that the ritual or meditation experience has run its course, bid farewell to the spirit and ask it to do work on your behalf. Then tell yourself that you will count backwards from five to one, and that when you reach one, you will be fully awake and relaxed carrying with you whatever power or spell you created in trance.

Ritually cleanse the space if you desire.

If you are patient and allot sufficient time to this practice—at least three times a week—the rewards will be great. The greatest barrier to get past is the tedium involved if the first few attempts don't meet your expectations. This *must* be ignored for a while. If you commit yourself to this practice for five days out of seven, by the end of the first week you will be pleased and surprised by the experience.

Patience and *commitment* are the keys to making this work.

CHAPTER ELEVEN

THE LORDS OF THE CROSSROADS

We begin with the single most important class of beings in any of the Voodoo pantheons. These personalities are so numerous and so vital to the practice of the magic that we have given them a chapter all their own.

The overall name for the spirit is *Eshu*, also called Eleggua, Elegba and (in Haiti) Legba, Kalfu and Baron Carrefour. These are one and all of the class of spirits that must be called upon at the beginning of any ceremony, for any purpose, if one expects results. They are trickster spirits with a childlike sense of humor and a childlike cruelty (the exception is the Haitian manifestation of Legba, who appears as an old man. In Africa he remains a strong sexual figure).

The family of Eshus are solar-phallic in nature, frequently pictured with an erect phallus, or some object that symbolizes the same. They are masters of doorways, roadways, crossroads (where the physical and the spiritual meet) and magic in general. They can be identified with the Greco-Roman Mercury (though not the dignified Thoth), and we have seen him convincingly compared to the Egyptian Set. He is often pictured as a young teenage boy, which should give you some idea of the sort of personality we are dealing with here.

His special day, according to *Santeria* and *Lucumi,* is Monday, although this kind of identification can vary (with all the spirits) depending not only on what country, but what *part* of what country you are in. The same variability applies to the saints that "mask" the spirits. For example, the saints used to disguise the spirits in New York are not always the same in Los Angeles or Brazil.

For Eshu the saint is often the Holy Child of Atocha, the Holy Guardian Angel, or St. Anthony. Colorful pictured candles are available for all of these. In Brazil the Eshus are identified with the Devil for reasons that will be explained. The colors of these spirits are black and red.

In Voodoo there are two different names for the spirits: *Orisha* (*Santeria/Lucumi*) and *Loa* (Haitian). They both refer to the emissaries of the creator god who were left on earth to interact with man. One of several names of this creator is Olodumare and, according to myth, when he finished his work he became disgusted with physical existence and went elsewhere; thus, he is not to be invoked since one would receive no response. The detailed legends of each of these "gods" will not be gone into here except cursorily as this has been done exhaustively in several other volumes easily available. Also, the stories tend to vary wildly, although the personalities and powers of the spirits do not.

What is important in this regard about Eshu (and his many brothers and sisters) is that because of a particular favor he did for the creator, Olodumare said that he would grant him any favor, he had only to tell him what it was. Eshu never hesitated: "I want," he said, "to do whatever I will." Olodumare granted this. So to this day, of all the spirits, the Eshus are free of restriction. They are openers of doorways and communication with the gods, flingers of the darkest kind of curse and bringers of death. This without punishment or guilt. Also, unlike the other spirits who rule over certain elements of the world and of life, they have no fixed kingdom. They go where they will and do as they please.

The magician is dependent on the good will of the Eshus to make a spell work. If he has incurred the enmity of one of these beings his efforts will fail and his luck will turn bad.

This spirit must be greeted and invoked whether he is the principle operator of the intended spell or not. Here is an example taken from the *Lucumi* tradition. As in many such invocations, the name of the spirit may be changed to the specific crossroad spirit invoked. It is not, however, a universal conjuration to be used with any spirit, but only with a representative of this class:

INVOCATION OF ESHU

> IBARAKOU MOLLUMBA ESHU IBACO MOYUMBA IBACO MOYUMBA. OMOTE CONICU IBACOO OMOTE AKO MOLLUMBA ESHU KULONA. IBARAKOU MOLLUMBA OMOLE KO IBARAKOU MOLLUMBA OMOLE KO. IBARAKOU MOLLUMBA AKO ESHU KULONA ACHE IBAKOU MOLLUMBA. ACHE ESHU KULONA IBARAKOU MOLLUMBA OMOLE KO AKO ACHE. ARONG LARO AKONG LAROLLE ESHU KULONA A ESHU COMA KOMIO ACHE. AKONKA LAR AKONKO LAR AKO ACHE IBA LA GUANA ESHU. LAROLLE AKONKO LARO LAROLLE E LAROLLE AKONKO AKNONKO LAROLLE AKONKO LAROLLE AKONKO LA GUANA E LAROLLE.

The language is corrupt *Yoruba*, called *Lucumi* in Cuba. It is easier to speak than it looks at first, since the chant is repetitive and quite musical. There are no tricks to pronunciation and the words are spoken as they appear. The "ache" referred to in the chant is the name of the primal vital force that is found in all magical traditions. It is the same as the "prana" of the yogis, or the "baraka" of the Arabs.

After any invocation it is customary to ask the spirit to do no harm to you or yours, and to play you no mischief in the execution of the spell. Those of you familiar with European magic will find this charge familiar.

There are several ways of representing one of these spirits during a ritual. The simplest comes from Haiti where an equilateral cross is drawn on the floor or ground with flour, corn meal or some similar substance. This is done with various flourishes and curlicues depending on the spirit invoked or the region in which the practitioners live (see, for example, the design for the shell divination board in this book). In the United States, where the Cuban form dominates, Eshu is usually called Eleggua or Elegba and is represented by a bust usually made from hand-molded concrete with eyes, ears and mouth of cowry shells. These figures are molded around a piece of doweling that is removed to leave a hollow cylindrical space in the bottom.

When *Santeria/Lucumi* was still primarily a rural practice, the head was "brought to life" by digging a hole in the center of a dirt crossroads and lowering the head into it. A rooster had its throat cut over the hole and the blood was drained onto the head. The rooster was laid into this hole and buried with the bust for a prescribed number of days.

Even among the most serious practitioners, this can be impractical in a modern urban setting. An alternative, which we have followed, is to purchase an unconsecrated bust at a botanica (if there is one in your city), perform a ritual involving the above invocation, the killing of a pigeon or other easily obtainable bird over the head, allowing the blood to dry, and asking the spirit of an Eshu to indwell the head. Seven stones or coins representing the seven sacred planets of ancient astrology, as well as the African powers connected to them, are placed in the hollow space and permanently sealed up with putty or concrete. When dry, the figure should be painted black (over the dried blood), except for the shell eyes and mouth, and the figure is "charged."

These "heads" are not expensive and are usually hand-made by *Santeros* who practice in the area. The heads come in various sizes from nearly that of a football to one that can fit in the palm of a hand and be easily hidden. The appropriate resting place for such a talisman is usually in a corner, a cabinet, or by a door. As always, the spirit should be asked through divination what part of the house it wants to live in. A direct answer should not be disregarded. This "personal" Eshu is responsible for your personal magical rituals and the guarding of your home. It should be given candy and (if it requests them) small toys, rum and cigars. For important ceremonies Eshu prefers the fresh blood of sacrificed fowl.

As an alternative, if you live in an area where there are no botanicas and don't want to try to mold things from cement, a fresh coconut can be obtained, the "top" cut off and the liquid poured out. Shells can be glued onto the "face" to represent eyes, nose, mouth and ears. Consecration can be done as above, but the seven stones should simply be dropped into the hollow interior. It need not be painted. When spells are cast requiring Eshu's help, the requests or talismans may be placed inside this hollow coconut head along with the proper rites.

In Brazil, Eshu is represented by the three-dimensional figure of a devil, often made of iron. He, or rather, they, are also represented by graphic sigils.

A selection of the literally hundreds of individuals in this family of spirits follows. Here are the twenty-one Eshus or Elegguas common in the *Santeria/Lucumi* tradition. To our knowledge these have been unpublished until recently. We obtained these names from a small booklet published by an Anglo who was initiated into the *Ifa* religion in Africa (*Esu— Elegba, Ifa and The Divine Messenger* by Awo Fa'lokun Fatunmbi, Original Publications, New York: 1992). Migene Gonzalez-Wippler has also published such a list, but the two do not match. We have selected this one partly arbitrarily and partly because of its (seeming) coherence.

Eshu Oro—Eshu of the power of the spoken word.
Eshu Opin—The guardian of sacred space.
Eshu Alaketu—Master of divine sensuality.
Eshu Iseri—Eshu of herbs and healing.
Eshu Gogo—Eshu of payment and justice.
Eshu Wara—Eshu of relationships.
Eshu Ijelu—Master of the drums.
Eshu Aiyede—Who brings messages from the spirits.
Eshu Odara—Lord of transformation.
Eshu Jeki Ebo Da—Eshu of sacred offerings.
Eshu Agongon Goja—Eshu of clothing or appearance.
Eshu Elekun—The hunter or predator.
Eshu Arowoje—Eshu for those who travel the ocean.
Eshu Lalu—Eshu of the dance.
Eshu Pakuta Si Ewa—Creator and destroyer of beauty.
Eshu Kewe Le Dunje—Eshu of sweets and sweetness.
Eshu Elebara—Eshu of power.
Eshu Emalona—Eshu of "any means necessary" or unusual measures.
Eshu Laroye—Messenger of the love goddess Oshun.
Eshu Ananaki—Eshu of remembrance of the past.

Eshu Okoburu—The divine enforcer. Okoburu is *Yoruban* for "wicked cudgel."

What follows is from the truly enormous Brazilian pantheon (or demonology) of Eshu. This is a mere selection, since these spirits have been named and dealt with in the hundreds upon hundreds in *Macumba* (or *Quimbanda*, if the magic is black). The sigils that accompany them may be drawn on the ground, used as talismans, or painted large to be concentrated on like a yantra.

ESHU REI

Eshu Rei, as the name suggests, is the "king Eshu," the most powerful master spirit of his class. He is to be called up only for major celebrations or operations. By reputation, if it appears at a ceremony without being called, considerable effort must be made to appease it and cause it to leave lest harm come to one and all. Conversely, if deliberately called, the reason had better be very good, and not some petty personal affair.

The safest and most beneficial way to deal with this enormous and dangerous being is to call him occasionally, offer sacrifice and ask for his general favor and that of his "family." His name can be used in invocations as a word of power to other Eshus, taking care to make it clear you are not actually calling *him*.

Invocation:

Naquela encruzilhada tem um rei
Esse rei e seu Tranca Gira
Na outra encruzilhada tem outro reino
E do Lucifer e de Pomba Gira

POMBA GIRA

Pomba Gira and her sisters are the female companions or colleagues of Eshu (wife or consort would be the wrong word). Pomba Gira means "spinning pigeon" because at *Quimbanda* ceremonies where she appears, the person possessed begins the manifestation by dancing and spinning drunkenly. The character of the Pomba Giras is for the most part lascivious, promiscuous, pleasure-loving and free of all inhibitions. She has much in common with the succubus of European demonology but without the sinister overtones. We say this bearing in mind that she still has the unpredictable personality of an Eshu.

She likes alcohol and sex and both can be indulged in her honor or used as an offering. She can be used to cause the satisfaction of love, or, perhaps more appropriately, lust and vice. In a more negative sense her power can be used to cause others to lose control and disgrace or ruin themselves.

Invocation:

Dona Pomba Gira e moca bonita da encruzilhada.
Ela vem, Ela vem, Ela vem
Firmar pontos na madrugada.
Ela deixou sua figueira
Tatare Eshu mulher.
Ela e Pomba Gira da encruza
A mulher de Lucifer.

ESHU TRANCA RUAS

Eshu Tranca Ruas specializes in aiding the magician in the blocking of the paths his enemies, or locking up their opportunities. He is to be invoked when the magician is in a competitive situation that he wishes or badly needs to win. Or when he becomes aware that someone is trying to harm him. The power of the spirit causes the focus of the spell to suffer from an inability to compete or to accomplish what he sets out to do without a hundred things going wrong.

Invocation:

Essa banda e de quimbanda
Essa banda lhe chamou
Bota fogo na fundanga
Derruba quem demandou.
Eshu e coroado rei
Viva Eshu Tranca-Rua
Seu ponto e seguro na encruzilhada
E ganga que vem de riba
firmar ponto na madrugada.
Eshu quer beber cachaca
Quer farofa na encruzilhada
Eshu quer ver Pomba Gira
Sambando na madrugada

ESHU MARABO

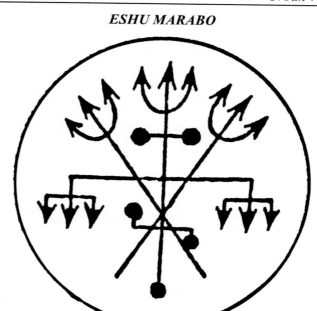

Eshu Marabo, like Eshu Tranca Ruas, is among the most "popular" of the Eshus. His powers tend to be general, bringing luck or harm, with the exception of the fact that he is known to specialize in illness. Not just in terms of causing it but also of healing it. These qualities do nothing to obviate the mercurial personality of his kind, and as always, care should be taken that he is pleased with his payment.

Invocation:

> *Poeira, poeira,*
> *Poeira de Eshu Marabo, poeira*
> *Poeira de Eshu Marabo, poeira*
> *Poeira da encruzilhada*
> *Poeira, poeira.*

ESHU DA CAPA PRETA

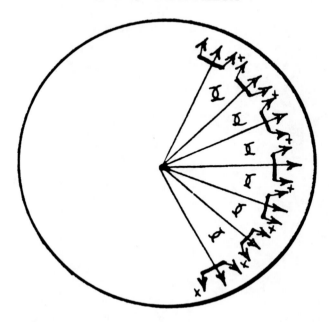

Eshu da Capa Preta is among the most sinister and dangerous of his family, specializing exclusively in the blackest magic. His name translates as "Eshu of the black cape". This conjures up images of Christopher Lee as Dracula.

Death curses, compulsions, psychic attack and spiritual slavery are all his stock in trade. Special care should be taken with the offering (use divination to find out what is desired) and with the ritual cleansing of the working space.

Invocation:

Eshu da Capa Preta
Com ele ninguem pode
Tem chifres como capeta
E barbicha como bode.

The invocations above are simple and should be repeated several times. In a *Macumba* ceremony they would be said or sung to the accompaniment of drums. Many of the names of the Eshus are corrupt *Yoruban* or Congolese, and at this point all but untranslatable. The invocations themselves are far from profound in translation, their value being, like Latin or Hebrew, that they have become "sacred" and the spirits recognize them when they hear them.

For example the invocation of Eshu Marabo translates as:

Dust, dust,
Dust of Eshu Marabo, dust
Dust of Eshu Marabo, dust
Dust of the crossroads
Dust, dust.

CHAPTER TWELVE

SOME OTHER MEMBERS OF THE FAMILY

The following are descriptions and sigils of many of the *Orishas* invoked in *Lucumi* and *Macumba*. The sigils are almost all Brazilian as this particular form of expression did not find fertile ground in Cuba. Bear in mind that each of the spirits, like the Eshus, have many "paths" or as we have put it, "members" of their family. If some variation of the classical description of the spirit appears, it does not imply failure or a mistake. You may have simply contacted one of the many "Changos" or "Oshuns".

THE IBEYI, OR SACRED TWINS—TAEBO AND KAINDE

Taebo and Kainde are the twin sons of Chango (the thunder god) and Oshun (the equivalent of Venus) whose descriptions follow. The twins are perpetually youthful, intelligent, playful and excellent at solving problems. They are particularly talented at curing illness, most particularly mental or emotional illness.

Taebo and Kainde are also good at causing luck at gambling, until they get bored, and are often appealed to in a situation where a "miracle" is needed. In such a situation, the supplicant creates an altar to the twins, with either the figures of two identical boys or a picture of St. Cosmo and St. Damian. Then a "party" is thrown in their honor, with cake, ice cream and anything else that children would like. This can take the form of an actual party with other guests if appropriate. If they are happy with the party, the miracle will occur.

It is appropriate to offer a blood sacrifice only if it is specifically requested. The correct offerings are usually identical plates of sweets or cakes left before their images or talisman.

Their colors are those of their parents, Chango and Oshun.

Invocation:
> *Vamos comer caruru, dois, dois.*
> *Na praia tem caruru.*
> *Vamos comer caruru, dois, dois.*
> *No bosque tem caruru.*
> *Vamos comer caruru, dois, dois.*
> *No terreiro tem caruru.*
> *Vamos chamar as criancas*
> *Pra comer munguaza*
> *Vamos chamar as criancas*
> *pra sarava no conga.*
> *Vamos chamar o Joaozinho*
> *Mariazinha e Cipriano*
> *Vamos chamar o Zezinho*
> *O Manezinho e o Mariano*

CHANGO

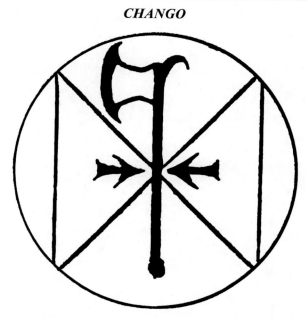

This most masculine and macho of spirits has been rather hilariously masked as the ethereal and feminine St. Barbara. This occurred simply because of the presence of Chango's symbols in her picture, just as St. Patrick became the mask of Dambalah in Haiti for no other reason than that there were snakes in the picture. His traditional image is that of a beautiful, very muscular man who carries a double-headed ax.

His colors are red and white and his day is Friday.

Chango is possibly the most popular of all the spirits and he is worshipped under the same name and with the same attributes from Los Angeles to Haiti. He can bring luck, love, strength (physical and moral) and sexual prowess. He likes to get drunk, but sometimes forbids his followers to do the same. He is also a womanizer and a talented magician hence his usefulness in love spells. He is a lord of thunder and fire and can cause storms and tempests.

His usual offerings include the sweetest, reddest apples that can be found, pomegranates and palm oil. Among the birds he prefers as blood offerings are roosters, turkey, and quail. He also accepts turtles.

Invocation:

> *Abrindo a minha engira*
> *Com Zambi e com Chango!*
> *abrindo a minha engira*
> *Com Zambi e com Chango!*
> *Sarava, seu Alafim!*
> *Sarava, seu Agoao!*
> *Sarava seu Alafim!*
> *Sarava seu Aganju!*

OSHUN

Oshun is the love goddess of the *Yorubas* and the patroness of gold. She is the mother of the Ibeyi twins and, because of her attributes, one of the most popular spirits. She is invoked in love spells, particularly by women, and by men in the acquisition of wealth. It is said that she is moody, and must be kept satisfied, or she will take away all she has given. If you have made a promise to her and do not keep it, you can make no greater enemy.

She also has power over that part of the human anatomy where the stomach, digestive tract and reproductive organs are located, thus, she is also appealed to in matters of fertility and any ailment of the stomach or colon.

Her colors are white and yellow, her day is Saturday, and her mask is the Virgin of Caridad del Cobre, the patroness of Cuba.

Her sacred place in nature, aside from the bedroom, is around fresh flowing water, such as rivers or streams. Offerings or spells done in her honor are especially effective if done at a river or stream. These should not be done by the ocean, as that is the kingdom of her sister Yemanja.

She is envisioned as a beautiful woman with copper-colored skin and long hair. Along with gold, her sacred metal is copper (which was also sacred to the Greek Venus).

Invocation:
Mamae Oshun
Papai Ogum Beira Mar
Estavam brincando na areia
Com o rosario de Iemanja
Arue minha mae
Minha mae me ensinou a nadar
Minha mae e raihna do mar
Tem areia, Tem areia
Adociaba no mar
Mamae Sereia.

OGUN

Ogun is the fighter-god, the war-god. He is lord of iron and patron of all conflicts and competitions. His mask is usually St. Peter (in Brazil it is St. George) and his day is Tuesday. He is lord of tools and weapons such as machetes and hammers.

His colors are green and black. For ordinary offerings he is fond of cigars and rum and his altar is decorated with miniature weapons and tools that are sold in most botanicas. In Brazil he is often portrayed as a roman soldier, and some similar figure would be an appropriate altar piece.

He is called upon to gain work for any matter regarding stone, metal or heavy machinery. He safeguards from accidents and like all spirits can also operate negatively in any of these areas.

Invocation:
Ogun, Ogun, de Timbire
Ogun de mana Zambe dao Luanda
As aves cantam quando ele vem de Aruanda
Trazendo pemba para salvar filhos de Unbanda
Oh japones, olha as costas do mar
Oh japones, olha as costas do mar.

OCHOSI, THE HUNTER

Ochosi is patron of hunters, birds and wild animals. He and his fellow hunter spirits are vital to any culture that lives off the land, and his like can be found the world over. In Brazil, figures of the various Ochosis look like native Indians, with steady eye and bow in hand. He is patron of hunters, birds and wild animals. His colors are violet, red, green and blue.

He is the leader of the "caboclos" or Indian spirits. In Voodoo the native elementals and the spirits of dead Indians are evoked as allies. This phenomenon even occurred in white American society during the advent of Spiritualism, when a number of famous mediums had "red Indians" as their spirit guides.

He has a number of masks, but our favorite is the one used in Brazil: St. Sebastian. Whether in the form of a statue or a print, Sebastian presents a wonderfully macabre figure, and demonstrates the frequent irony that the Catholic "mask" presents, since the arrows are *in* him rather than being shot *by* him. Stamped metal charms depicting a bow and arrow can be purchased at botanicas and carried as a talisman.

His offerings are toasted corn, palm oil, all game fowl and corn meal.

With his arrow representing the element of air, he is called upon magically to gain alertness and perception, to triumph in legal situations, and to send an "arrow" of psychic force against enemies. As a hunter he aids in finding things lost, stolen, or desired.

Invocation:

Eu tenho tres flechas
Tres flechas de guine
Uma e de Ochosi
Outra e de guine
E outra e pra quem quiser.

YEMANJA

Yemanja is the sea goddess. She is patroness of fertility and the abundance of life. In *Lucumi*, she is masked by Our Lady of Regla, but in Brazil where these spirits are far more publicly represented, she is pictured in statues and prints as either a mermaid or a woman dressed in pearls and blue robes.

Her colors are blue and white in *Lucumi* and crystal in *Macumba*. As offerings she accepts many types of fruits, especially watermelon. For animal offerings, pigeons and live fish and crustaceans are most easily obtainable.

In magic, she is called upon regarding any problem regarding the ocean and can give great wealth from the sea, protecting those who work on it. She is the ruler of all women's affairs and is patroness of women in general. She is also associated with the moon and has the attributes and gives the gifts common to moon goddesses.

Invocation:
Sou filho do mar.
Das ondas do mar
Da espuma do mar
Minlia mae Yemanja
O, Virgem Maria,
Como es linda flor,
Celeste harmonia,
Dulcissimo amor.
Manda em nossos lares
Rinha dos mares,
Da Terra e dos Ceus,
Em risos encobres.
Maria os seus dons,
Tesouro dos pogres
Riqueza dos bons.
Manda em nossos lares
Rainha dos mares,
Da Terra o dos Ceus.

CHAPTER THIRTEEN

COCAINE, ZOMBIES & CAULDRONS OF BLOOD: THE DARK SIDE

In nearly every recent account by sympathetic writers about Voodoo—whether Haitian or Cuban or Brazilian—great effort is made to point out that uninformed accounts of the subject malign it and the people who practice it. They say that the tales of altars running with blood and the casting of curses are the sensational accounts of ignorant journalists or religious bigots.

This is usually true. It is also true that these same books often end with tales of the very things they seek to play down. Like a priest's fondness for schoolboys or the proliferation of fundamentalist mental clinics, it's one of those things that is hard to completely ignore.

Most Americans have memories long enough to recall the invasion of Panama that garnered General Noriega's company in a federal prison. What most of us did not notice, because the various media covered it only fleetingly, was what the military discovered in the General's mansion after making the arrest.

When the army entered the house to collect evidence they found a large room dominated by a long table covered with glass-encased candles, strange statues, and little cloth bags among other obscure items. Upon examination, the bags were found to contain powder of various kinds and so they were taken for examination under the assumption that they were drugs. When analyzed, the powder was found to be an inert (from their point of view) mixture of herbs and incenses. The matter was largely forgotten, though it came out later that the General had, in his employ, one or more sorcerers of Brazilian, Cuban or Puerto Rican provenance.

The use of magic to attain and maintain power is not unusual. Americans know very little about it only because most journalists consider it irrelevant or are so ignorant they don't know what they are looking at when they see it. One of the recent presidents of Brazil (at least!) is said to have been a devotee of *Quimbanda*; and the Duvaliers of Haiti are well known to have practiced the black side of Voodoo and to have made alliances with its secret societies.

Related to the above, I (S. J. Black) have a story to relate told to me by a psychologist friend who went to Brazil just after "Baby Doc" Duvalier fled Port au Prince. He told me that the former members of the notorious *tonton macoute* had found a welcome haven in some parts of Brazil. Their off-shore bank accounts no doubt helped. At any rate, he swore to me that he had seen numbers of people who had either crossed them, or been poor workers in their employ (he didn't inquire too closely) in the "zombie" condition. The toxic formula described by Wade Davis in his book had been used on these people as was a formula of magical mind programming. He told me that he saw these people daily, carrying burdens (it was a rural area) or just standing around, utterly gone.

No secret was made of what had happened to these people, as it enhanced the prestige of the former enforcers and saved them the trouble of having to do it to too many others. I have never seen this story confirmed in any article or media report, nor would I particularly expect to. I have it from the person who claimed he saw it, and beyond that, I have no proof except that in many parts of the world, such a thing is far from unusual.

The late unlamented Idi Amin of Uganda was also known to have extensively employed black magicians. This was far more widely reported because ritual cannibalism was involved.

I have read a published account by a supposed witness who claims that Amin abducted someone who had offended him and that one of the most powerful and popular sorcerers-for-hire in Africa strapped him to a table and slowly skinned him alive during a ritual to capture his soul as a slave for Mr. Amin. His body was mummified and kept in a chest as the "link" to imprison his soul.

The immediate reaction by most people is that the above is the most scurrilous and ridiculous kind of rumor. I do not know if this particular story is absolutely true. What I _do_ know is that what I described is a genuine part of traditional African black magic that is practiced to this day. In fact, a little more than a year ago, television network news reported that helpless refugees from one of the African nations were being abducted and killed in just such ceremonies.

Not long ago, also nationally reported, the family of a Brazilian mayor was nearly lynched by a mob when it was discovered that they were part of a black magic circle responsible for the torture murder of a number of young children (probably by skinning, but they tried to keep the details quiet) and whose heads were then kept in cauldrons for use in magic. The news media kept referring to it as "satanic" but it was nothing of the sort, not in any historical sense. It was another dark form of Afro-Caribbean magic.

And this brings us to the world of _Palo Mayombe_.

Palo Mayombe (or _Palo Monte_) is magic that has its roots in the Congo region just as _Lucumi_ is basically _Yoruban_ and Haitian _Vaudun_ is basically Dahomean. It is by no means always black, but it always involves the remains of the dead, as it is beyond anything else, a technique of necromancy. Its initiated practitioners are called _Paleros_ or _Tata N'kisi_ (which means father of the spirits).

In Cuba, an elaborate initiation ceremony is performed wherein the aspiring sorcerer sleeps out of doors for a night and then digs up a corpse from a graveyard. The skull, flanges of the fingers, and tibia are removed and taken away to a ceremonial chamber where the spirit of the dead person is conjured.

I will not go into metaphysical speculation on whether a human soul can be bound after death.

If the spirit consents to serve the magician during his lifetime, a container is prepared for the human remains to serve as a "home." This is usually an iron cauldron filled with a bed of graveyard earth and other ingredients upon which the skull and other bones rest. "Primitive" as this sounds, the details of the arrangement make it clear that within the cauldron is created a microcosmic universe that could have been understood and appreciated by any renaissance hermeticist. This cauldron is called either a *nganga*, from the African, or a *prenda*, which is Spanish for "jewel", representing how precious it is.

Palo Mayombe is a complex and time-honored system of magic, and I would like to emphasize that the vast majority of *Paleros* absolutely do NOT participate in the kind of atrocity that I am about to describe.

Nearly ten years ago, a boy from Texas disappeared during a weekend drinking trip to Matamoros, Mexico with some of his college buddies. As a result of the search that followed, a mass grave was uncovered at an isolated ranch outside of town. The boy's body was there, as were many others. Eventually, the story came out that for many years, a powerful *Palero* from Florida had been working for the local drug-running families providing not only magical protection, but organizational services as well.

His name was Adolfo Luis Constanzo, and his full story is told in a fascinating book called *Buried Secrets* by Pulitzer prize winning author Edward Humes (Signet, New York: 1992). He was (according to himself) an initiated *Palero* of Cuban extraction who had been trained in blood magic since he was a child. This fantastic personality was personal advisor to some of Mexico's most famous and powerful people, from movie stars to high-level politicians.

He was also a monster who routinely skinned people alive on an altar in order to feed the spirit servitor in his bloody *nganga* pot. I have read several accounts of him and every author says repeatedly that the people who knew him insist that his spells "worked." What he foretold came to pass. If he did a spell for luck, your fortunes skyrocketed. Mr. Humes is a highly respected journalist, not a writer on "the strange world of psychic phenomena" yet he was clearly impressed by the consistency of these stories.

It becomes clear that Constanzo was a genuine psychic prodigy who was born into an environment where such talent could be focused and trained properly, and he used that ability like the sorcerers of old—to gain wealth and power. What was uncovered when he made the mistake of killing an American was a public horror, but what was even worse is the clear conclusion that if it was not for that error in judgment he might never have been caught or interfered with. He was almost a modern Gilles de Rais. It is amusing to compare the "magicians" and "witches" of American occult lodges with this powerful and wealthy monster.

In Florida, which has been the focus for the influx of Voodoo practitioners of all types, the police deal routinely with the involvement of professional black magicians in the drug trade. In Miami, gangland "hits" are often accompanied by *Vaudun* or *Lucumi* signs near the body. This is not to say that they were human sacrifices. They were the victims of crime rivalry with the added spice of having their souls captured or meddled with as additional punishment. *Paleros* and *Santeros* also do a heavy trade providing spiritual "luck" for cocaine traffickers.

It may surprise you that the fear of the werewolf is still very much a part of the modern world. The explorer and documentary film-maker Douchan Gersi in his book *Faces in the Smoke* (Jeremy P. Tarcher, Los Angeles: 1991) relates how he interviewed a number of people including military men who swore that they had caught and killed a lycanthrope that had been terrorizing the countryside. They told the classic story that when they cornered the beast it was in the form of a monster, but after death reverted to a man. Whatever the truth of the story, Mr. Gersi said that the wounds were real and the deaths caused by the "beast" were real. And on top of that he saw the corpse of the accused lycanthrope.

In Cuba, South America, Mexico and some parts of the southwestern U.S. this rumor still persists, with multiple witnesses and sometimes injuries and death to indicate that *something* happened. Those who are prepared to accept the efficacy of a spell or the operation of telepathy may draw the line at shape-shifting, but it is far better attested to than you might think. Most accounts indicate that the "wolf" isn't real, but an apparition that is nevertheless capable of doing harm. The sorcerer is often in a trance of some kind miles away, his spirit only in animal form. The writings of Carlos Castaneda also touch on this sort of thing.

The world is not what we are taught it is, and when the veil is pulled aside it can be weirder and more dangerous that anyone is willing to believe.

CHAPTER FOURTEEN

SPELLS

In this chapter we create a basic outline for the practical working of spells in the Voodoo tradition. Those familiar with the literature of magic will find that the basic ingredients and techniques are very little different from European witchcraft.

As this is intended to be a book that introduces outsiders to the practice of Afro-Caribbean magic, we will avoid much that is culturally specific or initially obscure. For example, the tradition of herbalism in all forms of Voodoo is truly enormous, and the majority of it is still passed along only by word of mouth. As an added complication, the names used for the herbs are different than those commonly used in the U.S., even when the names are in English.

Also note that there is no particular separation between, say, a Haitian technique or one of *Lucumi* origin. In New York and Florida, for example, there are Haitian immigrants who are initiates into *Santeria*, and *Santeros* who are also *Paleros*. Voodoo is about function and not artificial divisions based on meaningless sectarian symbolism. This, from our experience, seems to be one of the hardest things for people raised in a white Christian world to get past.

No *Bocor* or *Palero* would hesitate to use material from the *Key of Solomon* or any other European Grimoire if he thought it would work, and we urge you to take the same attitude. In this sense the Voodoo practitioner is the ultimate pragmatist.

While the principle focus of the book has been on spirit names of a *Yoruban* origin, there is no need to limit yourself to this.

The symbols used on the "board" created for the shell divination are Haitian. The symbol for Legba is related to the family of the Eshus, the symbol for Erzulie is related to Oshun, the symbol of Baron Samedi represents a spirit like Eshu Da Capa Preta and Erzulie Dantor is sister to Pomba Gira. Both Chango and Ogun are worshipped in Haiti under the same names and qualities.

To begin with, like all basic magic, these spells operate under the concept that what is similar to the mind or senses is similar in reality. This idea, ancient beyond calculation is the basis for the "doctrine of signatures" espoused by the Hermetic magicians and physicians of Europe.

THE SPELL OF ATTRACTION

First, it is important to create a link between the spell or force you are creating and its object or target. The closer the better. First in effectiveness are effluvia from the body itself; second, an object or article of clothing that the target has owned and carried for a long time; third a piece of writing or a signature and finally, a picture or simply an image in your mind.

Assuming that you have some sort of physical link—even a picture—take a container that is large enough to hold this link and place the object inside it. Along with this place a lodestone (commonly available at botanicas) or a small magnet that you can buy at any toy store. Cover these with honey. Next, invoke one of the lords of the crossroads and ask for help in contacting the forces necessary to make the spell work

Light a candle by the container and call upon the spirit to help in this operation. Take care that a proper offering is made. Always take the trouble to verbalize exactly what you want—and, if appropriate, why you want it—as though you were speaking to a person present in the room with you. Do not assume that the spirit is reading your mind.

Repeat this process for at least five days in a row, leaving the candle burning while you are in the house.

ANOTHER SPELL OF ATTRACTION

Similar to the above, but simpler, is to write the name of the desired lover on a piece if paper, and place it in a dish. Cover with honey or syrup while invoking Oshun and lighting a candle in her honor. Ideally the candle should be allowed to burn completely out, but if this is a safety hazard, keep it burning while you are at home. Don't blow the candle out. Snuff it out.

ANOTHER SPELL OF ATTRACTION

This spell is particularly useful in difficult cases, where you may want the love or good graces of someone who is unlikely to give it. Call on the Ibeyi twins, Taebo and Kainde, and offer them cakes and cookies. Talk to them of your problem and give them the name and description of the person to be influenced. Wait at least a day. Then take a small portion of the sweets and crumble it into a powder. Place this on the floor or pathway that the target of the spell must walk over, or hide it someplace where they spend time.

A SPELL OF ATTRACTION, LUST OR CONTROL

As described in the chapter on Eshu, obtain a fresh coconut, cut an opening in it, and remove the liquid. Glue shells to one side to create a face, or if these are unavailable use paint. Place the name and/or picture of the object of the spell within the hollow figure, and call upon the proper Eshu.

The spirit must be offered rum, candy and cigars. If the spell is particularly serious, the offering of a bird such as a pigeon may be made.

Broadly speaking, this spell may be used for any purpose regarding the influence or control of another, whether for love, lust, or defeat, all depending on the nature of the Eshu conjured. With this, as with other spells, time should be devoted to it. A candle should be burned by the figure and the conjuration and request made each night or day for a week or even longer.

TO CAUSE DISSENSION

Basically the same as the above, except that you need links for the two people between whom you wish to cause a falling out.

Place them in the container and cover with vinegar instead of honey, and call upon one of the more violent spirits, such as Eshu Da Capa Preta.

TO BLOCK SOMEONE'S PATH

Take a black candle, preferably molded in the shape of a person, and carve the name of the target of the spell upon it. Call upon Eshu Da Capa Preta and say that you give this person to him, that all of his affairs will fail and his efforts come to nothing. Explain to the spirit why this should be so, and do not question or qualify what may happen to the target. Release the spirit to take his pleasure upon this person and light the candle. Let it burn down, but save the remaining wax, either keeping it in your freezer as a magical imprisonment of his spirit, or burying it in a cemetery, leaving a small bottle of rum hidden as payment to the spirits of the graveyard.

TO REMOVE OR DESTROY AN ENEMY

Make or obtain a cloth Voodoo doll. Open it, and place within it a parchment with the person's name, as well as any magical link with the person that you might have. On top of this, sprinkle cayenne pepper, asafoetida, and (if you can get them) stinging nettles. If you wish you may also place the body of a wasp or scorpion inside. The doll should then be sewn up.

Select the appropriate spirit and call upon it to bring destruction upon or to remove the person. You may bind the doll with cord and keep it in a symbolic prison in your home, or you may hide or bury the doll in or near where the object of the curse works or lives. As a third alternative, it may be buried in a cemetery with a gift of rum for the graveyard spirits.

FOR DESTRUCTION OF AN ENEMY

Construct a miniature coffin of either cardboard or wood. Buy or construct a doll of wax, clay or cloth and unite it with a physical link belonging to the target. Place them in the coffin. Baptize the doll in the name of the person to whom you desire to do harm.

Call upon a death spirit such as Eshu Da Capa Preta or Baron Samedi and perform an impromptu funeral over the doll. At no time refer to it in any way other than as the person you wish to destroy. NEVER call it "the doll." Do this for three days in succession taking care to make the "funeral" as convincing as possible. At the end of the three days either bury the coffin (preferably in a cemetery) or cremate it. Expect results within a month. Remember, doing spells such as these are not actionable in U.S. courts.

TO CAUSE AN ENEMY TO DEPART

Obtain a quantity of graveyard earth, call upon the spirit you think is most appropriate and explain in detail why this person should be removed from your vicinity. Create a small shrine with a candle and an offering to the spirit. During the invocation, the graveyard earth should be "charged" with power.

The earth should be powdered finely and scattered over an area where the person is sure to walk. This can be either in or out of doors. The operation should be repeated for at least a week if practical and invocations for the desired effect done each night.

FOR MONEY AND PROSPERITY

Perform an invocation of Oshun. Use her colors (see the chapter on the spirits) and if possible candles with a picture of La Caridad Del Cobre, her Catholic mask. These are available at botanicas and many religious supply stores. Otherwise use green candles and anoint them with the money-drawing oil that can be obtained at any botanica or occult shop.

Place an appropriate offering to Oshun on a plate before the candles, and tell her of your needs and desires. Take a piece of silver or gold, or even a dollar, and anoint it with the money-draw oil. Place this in a envelope or mojo bag and carry it with you. Light the candles and say the invocation every night for at least a week and you will see your luck change.

FOR PROSPERITY

Select the appropriate spirit. Take a sum of money, preferably genuine silver (not the rubbish minted nowadays) or a piece of quality jewelry. Pour the blood of a sacrifice on the object in the name of the spirit, and place some of the blood on a talisman inscribed with the sign of the spirit. Carry the talisman on your person, and perform the invocation to the spirit at least three nights a week.

FOR A CLEANSING

This is done to rid yourself of bad luck or bad feelings. Cleanse the room in which you sleep by splashing the four quarters of the floor with "Florida water"—a mild, citrus smelling cologne that is available in botanicas and stores catering to a Latin clientele. It will not stain, and the clean, pleasant smell will soon evaporate. If this substance is not available, use incense or another cologne of your choice. The American Indian incense sage has also recently become widely available, and is traditionally used for this purpose.

Take either a live pigeon (if you consider the matter serious) or two eggs. Pass these over your body from your feet, over your head, down to the other side, and up and down the back and front of your torso. As you do this, ask the spirits to take the impurities from your spiritual and physical body. Then kill the bird by breaking its neck (do not cut its throat) and place it in a plain paper bag—or place the eggs in a paper bag with six pennies. Leave the bag at the corner of an intersection, unobtrusively against a building.

A LESSER CLEANSING AND SPELL OF PROTECTION

This is done in the name of Legba, Eleggua or one of the Eshus. Take the figure or sign of one of these beings—Legba's cross for example—and place it prominently in the place you wish to protect. Obtain a bottle of Florida Water or even holy water from a Catholic church. Perform the invocation to Eshu. Then, take the bottle of liquid and go around the space to be cleansed, sprinkling the substance very liberally. While doing this, visualize a barrier of white light blocking the entrance of all destructive influences and calling upon the spirits of the crossroads to guard you and reserve their mischief only for those persons or things that would cause you harm.

All of these spells are only simple outlines that can be expanded to much more elaborate versions. The most important element in this form of magic is direct communication with the spirit world, hence the emphasis earlier on various means of divination. Once these techniques are mastered, direct communication should provide you with instruction from the disembodied intelligences themselves, and you can dispense with the basic methods.

CHAPTER FIFTEEN

INITIATION & SELF-INITIATION

An important question regarding the practice of Voodoo and *Santeria* is the question of initiation. From our experience it is not easy for a person raised outside these traditions to become an *official* practitioner of either. This raises serious questions about the efficacy and safety of practice. Some theorists believe that one should only follow one's own tradition although one might *experiment* with other traditions. This last argument is very weak and reflects more a need for uniformity and stability than for safety and effectiveness.

The authors of this book have both been initiated into a number of esoteric groups which claim to practice magic. Both of us have experimented within these groups and observed their traditions. We found much of what is practiced there is an amalgam of many other traditions. Simply put, neither Mr. Black nor Dr. Hyatt have ever been initiated into a Wicca group, (thank God) yet we practice rituals which are similar to Wicca in our own work.

A prime example of an amalgam is the Hermetic Order Of The Golden Dawn which is regarded by some as the pinnacle of Western Esoteric Magic.

The first question to consider: is the Golden Dawn an original system—a thing in itself? The answer is "no." It, too, is an amalgam of numerous traditions, including Greek, Roman, Egyptian, Hebrew, and Christian.

The followers of the Golden Dawn attempt to defend it against the claim of being an amalgam of other traditions and systems by invoking its jewel, Enochiana, which was "channeled" by Mr. Kelly to Dr. Dee. This notion in and of itself is open to numerous questions and has been a topic of heated debate for many decades.

Regardless of the authenticity of the Enochian system, the entire history of the Golden Dawn is filled with forgery and fraud. This is true for many other systems as well. Entire books have been written from falsified papers, channeled "secrets" and by false prophets.

Even today many of the heads of various Golden Dawn Temples claim that they are the only legitimate "heirs." Of what one may ask? An illegitimate Order to begin with? However, with all this aside, the Golden Dawn itself is a workable system. If used properly it can help a student learn magic and aid him in his spiritual and personal development.

I have known hundreds of people who have been initiated into the Golden Dawn system. The authenticity of each initiation can be questioned because, as stated above, the origins of the Golden Dawn itself are questionable. More important than the "papers" each person holds are the results he or she has obtained. On this topic we have much less information.

If the Golden Dawn survives another few hundred years, new wonder stories will be created and the actual history will be ignored, much as the history of the Catholic Church is ignored. The same thing has happened with other forms of Christianity. Luther's illumination is sufficient as the inspirational component, and time has done the rest to make it legitimate. Often the proof of legitimacy—other than power and violence—is how long something has survived. The longer something has been around and is still functional, the more legitimate and holy it becomes. Our short life span makes it easy to fool us into believing things that are false. This is the major purpose of history—to time-bind events for the future from the perspective of the historian.

The question remains: are those individuals "formally" initiated into the Golden Dawn any better at what they do than someone who has practiced the work and forgone the initiation?

In this context the term "better" simply means "effective." We do not have an answer. We doubt that they are any "worse." But there is no doubt that some believe that without the link to the hidden masters—given in practice by pompous fools—the magic of the uninitiated is either evil or impotent.

Initiation implies a link with the etheric forces of an Order which is supposed to provide power and protection from otherwise dangerous forces. This is based on the assumption that the forces will recognize you if you possess the link. If the link is missing it is assumed that the practitioner, no matter how powerful, can get himself into trouble and is regarded as inauthentic, heretic and an outsider. Often the real purpose of initiation is to get the individual to believe in the wonder stories about the organization. It is often used just as it is in Christianity—as indoctrination. Step by step, grade by grade, in theory you are becoming more powerful, but ironically less dangerous to the Order's hierarchical structure.

There is no doubt that mistakes can be avoided by following the tried and true path. There is also no doubt that rarely is anything new or better created by following the tried and true path. The etheric question is one issue that can't easily be glossed over. Israel Regardie, one of the foremost experts in the field, felt that a properly done self-initiation was an adequate alternative to initiation by a group of individuals who had the "proper papers." Why?

Regardie said:

> In stating that the isolated student could now be his own initiator, one important phrase is rendered imperative. And that is he must be persistent and as thoroughgoing and exacting as if he were an initiator in a regularly constituted Golden Dawn temple under the constant scrutiny of officialdom and higher adept authorities. The responsibility for progress is thus placed inexorably on the student or candidate himself. As I see it—and I have watched this on a very few students—each elemental initiation or Watchtower ceremony requires its repetition several times. One student whom I am thinking of at this juncture has performed the whole...ceremonies some 50 or 60 times. It is therefore my opinion that she has

initiated herself as effectively and as positively as any temple initiatory hierophantic team could possibly do.[1]

The idea of degrees or papers must be kept separate from the issue of competency. I have known psychotherapists with no credentials who were more capable than most men of "letters." Credentials, however, do provide the sanction of the powers who have the authority to issue them which, for most people, *is more important* than competency.

The need for legitimacy is reflected in the maneuvers the founders of the Golden Dawn went through to create for themselves the correct papers to substantiate their wonder stories. (See *What You Should Know About the Golden Dawn*, Falcon Press, Tempe, AZ: 1993).

There is no doubt that papers are required to prove that you are good at what you do. Having legitimacy from an historical perspective is one means of demonstrating training and possibly competency. However, legitimacy and training are no guarantee of competency. I always look for a Doctor's diploma when I go to his office for treatment. After all, when I am sick I feel insecure and need some form of reassurance. However, my relationship with the physician is more important than his papers. I decide for myself whether he is able to deal with me and my difficulties, particularly if my life is at stake.

If I have a serious disease I always seek additional advice. I might even employ a psychic, or a practitioner of "alternative medicine." In these cases "papers" often mean nothing. As always, I rely on myself to determine the final answer. If I need surgery I would seek a surgeon whose reputation was based on his success-to-failure ratio and with whom I could communicate effectively.

However, when I do things for myself or my friends I do not ask to see my own papers. I rely on my own experience. Others, not knowing what I know of myself, feel better if they can see my papers. Sometimes I show them and other times I don't. It depends on my mood and the person who asks me. When I was in private practice I would alternate between putting my degrees

---

[1] *The Complete Golden Dawn System of Magic,* Falcon Press, Phoenix, AZ: 1984, Vol. 1, p. 9.

where they could be easily seen and putting them under my couch. The State finally demanded that all licenses be in plain view so I complied, but my University degrees were another matter. I knew one therapist who kept his degrees and license posted in his toilet. After all his experience and years in practice, this is what he finally felt about his diplomas and licenses as qualifications for working effectively with people.

Dr. Regardie had another point regarding self-initiation. He felt that some people are "called" to certain traditions. This can happen by "accident", or through a dream, a vision, a possession or an array of other "coincidences." In Regardie's discussion of self-initiation into the Neophyte grade of the Golden Dawn he concluded that,

> ...initiation outside of a regularly constituted Temple was only possible with two students. They would have to prove to themselves—not to anyone else—that they were wholly devoted to the Great Work, devoted enough to spend at least several months jointly or individually practising the Middle Pillar...

Dr. Regardie continues on by emphasizing,

> ...If this practice were assiduous and intense both students would have awakened in themselves the psycho-spiritual energy that could not only hasten their own inner development but that the latter could be communicated to yet another in a manner not too dissimilar to that described in Z–3.
>
> The fundamental requirement was that the initiator should be an initiator—not a layman out of the brute herd. Something must have happened to him to have redeemed him of the stigma of being 'ordinary.' Of course it would have been better if he (or she) had been the recipient of a spontaneous mystical experience of the type described in James... Since this kind of attainment cannot be made to order, as it were, the only alternative is to fall back on time honored methods of development and growth.[1]

---

[1]*Op. cit.*, pp. 10–11.

Mr. Black and I have had numerous mystical experiences and, combined with our own personal and joint workings, feel that we meet the criterion laid down by Dr. Regardie at least in terms of the practice of Western Voodoo. (We need to call it Western Voodoo or Urban Voodoo so as not to deceive ourselves or anyone else. Both of us are from the Western Esoteric tradition and between us have close to fifty years of practice. Thusly, our style of Voodoo reflects our origins as well as our experiences.)

Sometimes special people can't receive initiation or do not want it because of their intense natures. They are rogues who must go it on their own. Others find initiation very difficult. They do not like groups or attending meetings. This means they, too, go it alone. They buy books, study, practice, make mistakes, innovate and come up with their own system. Between the good material available today, and other rogues with whom to share experiences and learn, it is not necessary to seek organized forms of initiation. While I have taken the route of the rogue in some instances, in other cases I have gone through the normal process of initiation. There were many reasons behind taking formal initiations. In one case it was out of respect for my teacher; in others it was to see what was behind the veil. Unfortunately, more often than not, there was nothing.

One problem with "the going it alone route": if you later require acknowledgment of your expertise from these groups, you will rarely get it even if you are really good—and sometimes because you are *too* good. If you do receive some acceptance, you will often be treated as an outsider, unless of course you are so powerful you can "storm the temple" and take it over.

Some groups, particularly when they are starting up, will accept degrees or levels of initiation from other groups. This is rare and still requires some sort of initiation into the new group.

Insiders and outsiders has always been an important issue for anthropologists and sociologists. Usually they attempt to interpret these issues in a utilitarian fashion. Often, however, they miss the point.

Outsiders have always been the innovators, the creators of new systems and the rejuvenators of older systems. Every successful rebel (see *Rebels and Devils: The Psychology of Liberation*, edited by Christopher S. Hyatt, with contributions by

William S. Burroughs, Robert Anton Wilson, Timothy Leary, et. al., (Falcon Press, Tempe, AZ: 1995) becomes the new dictator who later is overcome by new and more vibrant forces.

If one chooses to become initiated into a "alien" tradition, he will by necessity have to go through the ordeals set by his teachers. I have done it in many ways. I have had traditional initiations, semi-traditional initiations and none at all. One effect of traditional initiation is the imprint created in the mind. For me this had lasting importance in some cases, but so did my first love affair. I have created similar effects on my own or with a few associates who I trusted.

Being a legitimate member of a group allows one to feel superior to outsiders as well as to climb the hierarchy by passing exams, biding one's time and being in favor with the authorities.

In Voodoo, however, results achieved by reputation are more important than "passing exams" and attending empty formalities. The same holds true for those who are unfortunately called "fortune tellers." Reputation and results can often override degrees, diplomas or initiations.

What is important is integrity, a sense of calling, and lots of practice—which, of course, implies lots of mistakes. Knowing when you made a mistake is much harder to determine in the practice of magic than in surgery. Sometimes the results you want from a magical operation bring a lot of discomfort and anxiety. Things might well work out in the end, but the process of getting there can at least be said to be exciting. Mr. Black and I have had numerous experiences which seem to indicate that we had made an error but after a period of discomfort which often motivates us further we have more often than not found out that we were on the right path after all.

The practice of Voodoo demands that a person own his actions. This is no different from the performance of any type of *real* magic. The concept of personal responsibility is particularly true when the practitioner does not belong to a community—it is easy to blame the group or the teacher. This aside, the solitary practitioner must alone decide on the value of his rituals and actions. There is no community, no priest, no doctor or official.

For many modern men this is horrifying since they are used to hiring priests and others, not only to do their work for them, but to blame for their own disowned desires.

For example: a greedy man wants more money, so he hires a broker but the broker fails. The rage is aimed at the broker not only for his failure but because of the man's own greed. The motive becomes intertwined with the methods designed to satisfy the greed. The result is to blame the broker.

The same is true when we refuse to take responsibility for revenge. A person with integrity doesn't take revenge on the beautiful simply because he is less beautiful. This type of person is the Christian. One must have the utmost integrity to take revenge in a constructive way. If you are unhappy because of what you are, change, or learn to transform yourself. Don't blame a better man for your weakness. Blame instead the slave mentality which permeates the entire world.

A METHOD OF SELF-INITIATION

For a person who wishes to practice Voodoo and doesn't want initiation or can't find a suitable means we present a method which has worked for us. Keep in mind that you must decide what you can or can't tolerate. We are not responsible for what you do. You paid for this book—as such you paid for our experiences and knowledge. What you do with this book is up to you—it is your responsibility. Remember, even though there are millions of people who follow Voodoo, this is no justification for irresponsible actions. You must decide how serious you are and how much suffering you might be willing to tolerate.

An intensive set of divinations are first necessary. Set up a circle, prepare an altar, perform a sacrifice, obtain equipment, purify yourself, play music, listen to sounds, choose colors, buy an image, prepare a talisman, perform a ritual at least once a week for a month. Pay attention to dreams, coincidences, etc. Keep a journal of your practices.

Without benefit of a "real" *Santero* or *Houngan* to initiate you, there is another tradition of far greater age that can be adapted to the purpose for the serious student.

According to shamanic lore, a person who has reason to believe that he has been "called" to the practice of magic often goes into the forest by himself and, by use of spontaneous trance states, learns the arts of magic from the spirits themselves. In other words, they go off by themselves in a state of ignorance and return with a body of knowledge obtained from persons or things unknown. Parallels to this exist in every religious tradition including the Christian.

Since we are discussing "Urban Voodoo," going on a pilgrimage into the forest may be inconvenient, so we have here a simple method based on tradition. Its principle requirements are a commitment of time and a serious willingness to a rather scary form of psychic openness.

For this you will need a very simple small devotional space or altar. You will also need some form of crossroad spirit like an Eleggua who will be the person you will principally address.

You should cover this space with a white cloth and have at least one glass-encased candle and perfumed oil or Florida water to anoint the figure or sigil.

This exercise should be done both morning and evening. Begin with a ritual bath or washing. When the water is drawn, say this over it:

LORD GOD ADONAY, WHO HAST CREATED MAN FROM EARTH TO REFLECT THINE OWN IMAGE AND LIKENESS, WHO HAS CREATED ME ALSO, UNWORTHY AS I AM, DEIGN, I PRAY THEE, TO BLESS THIS WATER THAT I MAY BE HEALTHFUL TO MY BODY AND SOUL, THAT ALL DELUSION AND ILL WILL MAY DEPART FROM ME. O LORD GOD, ALMIGHTY AND INEFFABLE, WHO DIDST LEAD THY PEOPLE FORTH FROM THE LAND OF EGYPT, AND DIDST CAUSE THEM TO PASS DRY-SHOD OVER THE RED SEA! GRANT THAT I MAY BE CLEANSED BY THIS WATER FROM ALL MY IMPIETIES AND MAY APPEAR BLAMELESS BEFORE THEE. AMEN.

Immerse yourself in the water and imagine all mental and physical impurities washed away.

Approach the altar and invoke Legba/Eshu. Ask for an introduction to the spirits and the ability to speak with them. Use the techniques of self-hypnosis to open yourself to this. Then retire to bed. Keep a dream diary for the night.

This same technique can be performed in the morning, asking for signs of the spirit's presence. This sounds deceptively simple, but if you pursue it for a month or more, you will be startled by the results.

A word of warning: you should also be prepared to have experiences that may prove frightening, but if you have the courage to endure these, you will find yourself greatly rewarded and your life changed for the better.

FROM CHRISTOPHER S. HYATT, Ph.D.

SECRETS OF WESTERN TANTRA
The Sexuality of the Middle Path

Introduced by J.M. Spiegelman, Ph.D.
Preface by Robert Anton Wilson

Dr. Hyatt reveals secret methods of enlightenment through transmutation of the *orgastic reflex*. Filled with explicit, practical techniques.

"The world's first scientific experimental yoga that does not expurgate the sensory-sensual-sexual aspects of the Great Work."
— Robert Anton Wilson

SEX MAGICK, TANTRA & TAROT
The Way of the Secret Lover

With Lon Milo DuQuette
Illustrated by David P. Wilson

A wealth of practical and passionate Tantric techniques utilizing the Archetypal images of the Tarot. Nothing is held back. All methods are explicit and clearly described.

"Each of us has a Guardian Angel — a companion and lover who waits just behind the images that flood our minds during sleep or reverie."

THE PSYCHOPATH'S BIBLE
For the Extreme Individual

Foreword by Nicholas Tharcher

Throughout time, psychopaths have gotten a bad rap since almost all of the world's religious and social philosophies have little use for the individual—except as a tool to be placed in service to "God," or the "collective," or the "higher good" or some other equally undefinable term. Here, finally, is a book which celebrates, encourages and educates the best part of ourselves — The Psychopath.

TO LIE IS HUMAN
Not Getting Caught Is Divine

Introduced by Robert Anton Wilson

Take a tour of the prison erected by the lies that society tells you...and the lies you tell yourself. Then, learn the tools to tunnel out...

"Is it possible to use language to undo the hallucinations created by language? ...a few heroic efforts seem able to jolt readers awake... to transcend words."
— Robert Anton Wilson

THE *Original* FALCON PRESS

Invites You to Visit Our Website:
http://originalfalcon.com

At our website you can:

- Browse the online catalog of all of our great titles
- Find out what's available and what's out of stock
- Get special discounts
- Order our titles through our secure online server
- Find products not available anywhere else including:
    – One of a kind and limited availability products
    – Special packages
    – Special pricing
- Get free gifts
- Join our email list for advance notice of New Releases and Special Offers
- Find out about book signings and author events
- Send email to our authors
- Read excerpts of many of our titles
- Find links to our authors' websites
- Discover links to other weird and wonderful sites
- And much, much more

Get online today at http://originalfalcon.com

- The Gods Return -
-Bobby Hemmitt -